Activities for the
Differentiated
Classroom

Gayle H. Gregory • **Carolyn Chapman**

CORWIN PRESS
Classroom

For information:

Corwin Press
A SAGE Publications Company
2455 Teller Road
Thousand Oaks, California 91320
CorwinPress.com

SAGE, Ltd.
1 Oliver's Yard
55 City Road
London EC1Y 1SP
United Kingdom

SAGE India Pvt. Ltd.
B 1/I 1 Mohan Cooperative
Industrial Area
Mathura Road, New Delhi
India 110 044

SAGE Asia-Pacific Pvt. Ltd.
33 Pekin Street #02-01
Far East Square
Singapore 048763

Printed in the United States of America.

ISBN 978-1-4129-5340-5

This book is printed on acid-free paper.

08 09 10 11 10 9 8 7 6 5 4 3 2 1

Executive Editor: Kathleen Hex
Managing Developmental Editor: Christine Hood
Editorial Assistant: Anne O'Dell
Developmental Writer: Sally Griffith
Proofreader: Bette Darwin
Art Director: Anthony D. Paular
Cover Designer: Monique Hahn
Interior Production Artist: Karine Hovsepian and Lisa Riley

Activities *for the* Differentiated Classroom

GRADE **4**

TABLE OF CONTENTS

Connections to Standards 4

Introduction 6

Put It Into Practice 7

CHAPTER 1
Mathematics 9
Activities and reproducibles

CHAPTER 2
Science 23
Activities and reproducibles

CHAPTER 3
Social Studies 42
Activities and reproducibles

CHAPTER 4
Language Arts 60
Activities and reproducibles

CHAPTER 5
Physical Education, Art, and Music 79
Activities and reproducibles

References 96

Connections to Standards

This chart shows the national academic standards covered in each chapter.

MATHEMATICS	Standards are covered on pages
Numbers and Operations—Understand numbers, ways of representing numbers, relationships among numbers, and number systems.	13
Geometry—Use visualization, spatial reasoning, and geometric modeling to solve problems.	18, 20
Measurement—Apply appropriate techniques, tools, and formulas to determine measurement.	17
Data Analysis and Probability—Select and use appropriate statistical methods to analyze data.	22
Problem Solving—Solve problems that arise in mathematics and in other contexts.	16
Problem Solving—Apply and adapt a variety of appropriate strategies to solve problems.	9
Problem Solving—Monitor and reflect on the process of mathematical problem solving.	10, 12
Reasoning and Proof—Develop and evaluate mathematical arguments and proofs.	15

SCIENCE	Standards are covered on pages
Science as Inquiry—Understand about scientific inquiry.	23
Physical Science—Understand properties of objects and materials.	26
Physical Science—Understand light, heat, electricity, and magnetism.	25, 27, 28
Life Science—Understand characteristics of organisms.	31
Life Science—Understand organisms and environments.	31, 34
Earth and Space Science—Understand properties of earth materials.	37
Science in Personal and Social Perspectives—Understand changes in environments.	35
History and Nature of Science—Understand science as a human endeavor.	38, 41

SOCIAL STUDIES	Standards are covered on pages
Understand culture and cultural diversity.	59
Understand the ways human beings view themselves in and over time.	47, 57
Understand interactions among people, places, and environments.	47
Understand individual development and identity.	42
Understand interactions among individuals, groups, and institutions.	47, 57
Understand how people create and change structures of power, authority, and governance.	56
Understand how people organize for the production, distribution, and consumption of goods and services.	49, 54
Understand the ideals, principles, and practices of citizenship in a democratic republic.	51, 52

LANGUAGE ARTS	Standards are covered on pages
Read a wide range of literature from many periods in many genres to build an understanding of the many dimensions (e.g., philosophical, ethical, aesthetic) of human experience.	62
Apply a wide range of strategies to comprehend, interpret, evaluate, and appreciate texts. Draw on prior experience, interactions with other readers and writers, knowledge of word meaning and of other texts, word identification strategies, and understanding of textual features.	60, 63, 66, 73
Apply knowledge of language structure, language conventions (e.g., spelling and punctuation), media techniques, figurative language, and genre to create, critique, and discuss print and nonprint texts.	76, 78
Develop an understanding of and respect for diversity in language use, patterns, and dialects across cultures, ethnic groups, geographic regions, and social roles.	75
Participate as knowledgeable, reflective, creative, and critical members of a variety of literacy communities.	69
Use spoken, written, and visual language to accomplish a purpose (e.g., for learning, enjoyment, persuasion, and the exchange of information).	65, 71

Introduction

As a teacher who has adopted the differentiated philosophy, you design instruction to embrace the diversity of the unique students in your classroom and strategically select tools to build a classroom where all students can succeed. This requires careful planning and a very large toolkit! You must make decisions about what strategies and activities best meet the needs of the students in your classroom at that time. It is not a "one size fits all" approach.

When planning for differentiated instruction, include the steps described below. Refer to the planning model in *Differentiated Instructional Strategies: One Size Doesn't Fit All, Second Edition* (Gregory & Chapman, 2007) for more detailed information.

1. Establish standards, essential questions, and expectations for the lesson or unit.

2. Identify content, including facts, vocabulary, and essential skills.

3. Activate prior knowledge. Pre-assess students' levels of readiness for the learning and collect data on students' interests and attitudes about the topic.

4. Determine what students need to learn and how they will learn it. Plan various activities that complement the learning styles and readiness levels of all students in this particular class. Locate appropriate resources or materials for all levels of readiness.

5. Apply the strategies and adjust to meet students' varied needs.

6. Decide how you will assess students' knowledge. Consider providing choices for students to demonstrate what they know.

Differentiation does not mean always tiering every lesson for three levels of complexity or challenge. It *does* mean finding interesting, engaging, and appropriate ways to help students learn new concepts and skills. The practical activities in this book are designed to support your differentiated lesson plans. They are not pre-packaged units, but rather activities you can incorporate into your plan for meeting the unique needs of the students in your classroom right now. Use these activities as they fit into differentiated lessons or units you are planning. They might be used for total group lessons, to reinforce learning with individuals or small groups, to focus attention, to provide additional rehearsal opportunities, or to assess knowledge. Your differentiated toolkit should be brimming with engaging learning opportunities. Take out those tools and start building success for all your students!

Put It into Practice

Differentiation is a Philosophy

For years teachers planned "the lesson" and taught it to all students, knowing that some will get it and some will not. Faced with NCLB and armed with brain research, we now know that this method of lesson planning will not reach the needs of all students. Every student learns differently. In order to leave no child behind, we must teach differently.

Differentiation is a philosophy that enables teachers to plan strategically in order to reach the needs of the diverse learners in the classroom and to help them meet the standards. Supporters of differentiation as a philosophy believe:

- All students have areas of strength.
- All students have areas that need to be strengthened.
- Each student's brain is as unique as a fingerprint.
- It is never too late to learn.
- When beginning a new topic, students bring their prior knowledge base and experience to the new learning.
- Emotions, feelings, and attitudes affect learning.
- All students can learn.
- Students learn in different ways at different times.

The Differentiated Classroom

A differentiated classroom is one in which the teacher responds to the unique needs of the students in that room, at that time. Differentiated instruction provides a variety of options to successfully reach targeted standards. It meets learners where they are and offers challenging, appropriate options for them to achieve success.

Differentiating Content By differentiating content the standards are met while the needs of the particular students being taught are considered. The teacher strategically selects the information to teach and the best resources with which to teach it using different genres, leveling materials, using a variety of instructional materials, and providing choice.

Differentiating Assessment Tools Most teachers already differentiate assessment during and after the learning. However, it is equally important to assess what knowledge or interests students bring to the learning formally or informally.

Assessing student knowledge prior to the learning experience helps the teacher find out:

- What standards, objectives, concepts, skills the students already understand

- What further instruction and opportunities for mastery are needed

- What areas of interests and feelings will influence the topic under study

- How to establish flexible groups—total, alone, partner, small group

Differentiating Performance Tasks In a differentiated classroom, the teacher provides various opportunities and choices for the students to show what they've learned. Students use their strengths to show what they know through a reflection activity, a portfolio, or an authentic task.

Differentiating Instructional Strategies When teachers vary instructional strategies and activities, more students learn content and meet standards. By targeting diverse intelligences and learning styles, teachers can develop learning activities that help students work in their areas of strength as well as areas that still need strengthening.

Some of these instructional strategies include:

- Graphic organizers

- Cubing

- Role-playing

- Centers

- Choice boards

- Adjustable assignments

- Projects

- Academic contracts

When planning, teachers in the differentiated classroom focus on the standards, but also adjust and redesign the learning activities, tailoring them to the needs of the unique learners in each classroom. Teachers also consider how the brain operates and strive to use research-based, best practices to maximize student learning. Through differentiation we give students the opportunity to learn to their full potential. A differentiated classroom engages students and facilitates learning so all learners can succeed!

CHAPTER 1

Mathematics

Don't Make Students Bored!

Standard
Problem Solving—Apply and adapt a variety of appropriate strategies to solve problems.

Objective
Students will use mnemonic devices to help remember the steps used in the long division process.

It's challenging to continue motivating students day after day, especially when teaching a process such as long division. One differentiated instructional strategy that can help is *rehearsal*, the act of processing in working memory. Mnemonics is a rehearsal strategy that associates easily remembered phrases with information students need to retrieve.

The steps of the long division process can be difficult to remember. First, you divide, then multiply, then subtract, and finally bring down what's left of the dividend. A common mnemonic device for this process is *Dad, Mother, Sister, Brother.* However, it's much more motivating for students to create their own mnemonic devices. This activity engages students' creativity and supports verbal/linguistic and logical/mathematical learners.

Challenge students to see how many mnemonic devices they can invent. To get started, invite them think of people to whom they might write a letter. For example: *Dear Mr. Sponge Bob* or *Dear Ms. Sandra Bullock.* They can also connect mnemonics to classmates or someone who works at your school. Invite students to be creative and brainstorm silly mnemonics as well, such as *Dogs Might Steal Bacon, Dolls Must Smile Brightly,* or *Donuts Make Sloppy Bellies.*

Ideas for More Differentiation
Before starting a math assignment, have students draw four boxes in the top right corner of the page. In each box, have them write or draw a symbol for each step of the process, while reciting the mnemonic device. This is an especially good strategy for visual learners.

Strategies
Rehearsal

Mnemonics

Rainbow Division

Standard

Problem Solving—Monitor and reflect on the process of mathematical problem solving.

Objective

Students will monitor the processes of long division by using colored lines to organize their thinking.

Materials

notebook paper

colored pencils or fine-line markers

Do you have students who get lost while doing long division? Rainbow division is a strategy that helps students stay focused during each step of the process. Because the strategy uses colors and lines, it especially appeals to visual/spatial learners.

1. Have students set up their papers by writing the word *multiply* or the multiplication sign at the top of the left margin. Students will solve the multiplication steps for their division problems in this section of the paper only. This keeps the page organized and prevents a certain amount of messiness.

2. Ask them to write a mnemonic device (e.g., *DMSB*) or four boxes with the signs for *divide*, *multiply*, *subtract*, and *bring down* (see page 9) at the top right corner of their paper.

3. Have students copy their first long division problem and draw a box around the divisor.

4. Tell students to use red marker to draw a rainbow-shaped arc from the divisor in the box to the first numeral in the dividend. Students think to themselves: *Does the divisor go into this first number?* If it doesn't, they use orange marker to draw an arc from the divisor to the second number in the dividend. They now think: *Does the divisor go into this second number?* If it doesn't, students use yellow marker to draw an arc from the divisor to the third number in the dividend.

5. Have students continue in this manner using the colors of the rainbow in order (red, orange, yellow, green, blue, and purple), until the divisor does go into the dividend. Students then write the first numeral of the quotient in the correct place (the arc helps show where to write it).

6. Students continue working the problem by multiplying in the multiplication column, subtracting, and starting over again with the divisor. This time, they draw a red arc from the bottom of the divisor box to the new number. If the number does not go in, they use the orange marker to draw an arc, and maybe bring down the next number. Students continue drawing rainbows and following the steps until they solve the problem. There may be many rainbows on each problem!

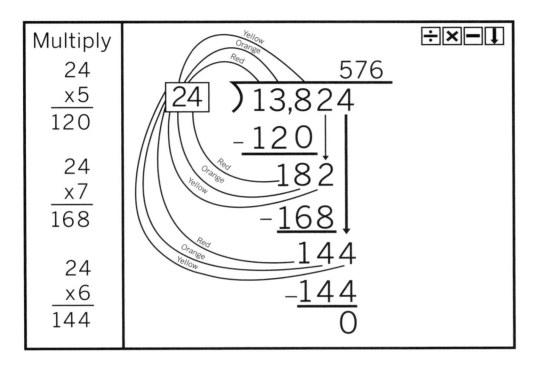

Ideas for More Differentiation

Encourage students to remember the order of rainbow colors using the mnemonic *ROY G. BIV* (red, orange, yellow, green, blue, indigo, and violet).

Color-Coded Multiplication

Strategy
Multiple intelligences

Standard
Problem Solving—Monitor and reflect on the process of mathematical problem solving.

Objective
Students will color-code the steps in long multiplication in order to keep organized.

Materials
notebook paper
colored pencils or fine-line markers

When students do multiplication, they often get incorrect answers because they write the products in the wrong places. Or, they get mixed up when carrying the numbers in the tens and hundreds places and add numbers they've already used. A simple way to help students monitor these steps is to color-code each step. This activity especially appeals to visual learners.

Note: The number of steps will vary according to the multiplication problem. The following steps demonstrate a three-digit number multiplied by a three-digit number.

1. Have students use a red marker to write the product from multiplying the numbers in the ones place. They also use a red marker to write the numbers they carry.

2. Ask students to use an orange marker to write the product from multiplying the numbers in the tens place and the numbers they carry. (Using orange makes ignoring the red numbers they already used much easier.)

3. Have students use a green marker to write the product from multiplying the numbers in the hundreds place and the numbers they carry. (This time, they ignore the orange numbers they already used.)

4. Finally, students use blue marker to add the products for the final answer.

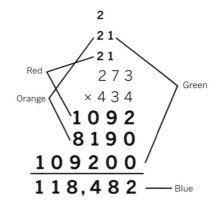

What's in a Name?

Standard

Numbers and Operations—Understand numbers, ways of representing numbers, relationships among numbers, and number systems.

Strategies
Focus activity

Metaphor/analogy

Objective

Students will practice giving equivalent fractions different names.

Try this focus activity to help students open their mental files before a lesson on equivalent fractions.

1. Introduce the activity by telling students that equivalent fractions represent the same number, just as the word *teacher* as well as your title and last name represent you in the classroom. You may go by other names as well, such as *Mom, Honey, Maria,* and *Coach.* Explain that we all have many titles that represent who we are. The names may be different, but we are the same people.

2. Invite students to brainstorm a list of all their names. They can think of their nicknames, the names their brothers or sisters call them, the names their parents or grandparents call them, and more. The only rule is that the names have to be classroom appropriate! Invite students to share their names with a partner.

3. Call a volunteer to the front of the class. Introduce the student using all of his or her names, for example: *This girl is known to all of you as Kristy. She is also known as Cookie to her brother, Sweet Pea to her parents, and Kris to her grandparents. Her friends on the soccer team call her Animal. Kristy is the same person in the classroom as she is when she's at home or on the soccer field. She doesn't change, although she may look a little different in her school clothes and her soccer uniform.*

4. Explain that our names are like equivalent fractions. The fraction *1/2* is the same as the fractions *2/4* and *4/8.* The fractions represent the same amount; they just have different names and look a little different.

5. Draw three pie charts on the board. Divide the first one to show *1/2*, the next one to show *2/4*, and the last one to show *4/8*. Point out that all the fractions represent the same amount. Tell students: *We can call our friend Kristy 1/2, 2/4, or 4/8, but she is still Kristy. Or, we can call half of this pie Cookie, Sweet Pea, or even Animal, but it is still half of a pie!*

Ideas for More Differentiation

Give each student an index card, and assign him or her a fraction (make sure to include several equivalent fractions). Ask students to illustrate their fraction on the card by drawing simple pictures, such as a pie divided into six pieces with three pieces shaded. Invite students to get out of their seats and mingle amongst each other to find their matching equivalent fractions (e.g., *3/6, 1/2, 4/8, 6/12, 5/10*). Have students form groups of equivalent fractions. Encourage them to discuss and agree on whether each student belongs in the group. When all groups have come to consensus, ask them to share their equivalent fractions with the class.

Factions for Fractions

Standard
Reasoning and Proof—Develop and evaluate mathematical arguments and proofs.

Objective
Students will create a representation of a given fraction and three equivalent fractions and present their creations to the class.

Materials
12"x 18"construction paper
construction paper scraps
glue
scissors
crayons

Invite students to show what they've learned about equivalent fractions by creating either two- or three-dimensional figures. Working in cooperative groups of three, have students make an object that demonstrates its equality to the other objects in the group. For example, a group has the fraction 2/3. One group member makes a construction paper pizza that shows 2/3. Another makes a pizza that shows 4/6, and the last student makes a pizza that shows 8/12. When presenting each pizza to the class, group members can lay one on top of the other to show that they are equal in size even though they are segmented into different pieces.

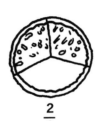
$\frac{2}{3}$

$\frac{4}{6}$

$\frac{8}{12}$

Encourage students to develop social skills within their cooperative groups by deciding the following:

- What will they make to show the equivalent fractions (e.g., pizzas, cookies, oranges, chocolate bars, birthday cakes, pies)?

- What should they use as a template, since all figures must be the same size in order to be accurate? (The pizza group might have used the base of a trashcan to trace circles.)

- Who will do each job? Some suggestions include:
  - Reporter (presents findings to the class, although the others may help)
  - Researcher (finds the equivalent fractions)
  - Quality Controller (makes sure the job is being done correctly)

One for You, Half for Me?

Strategies

Cooperative group learning

Authentic task

Standard

Problem Solving—Solve problems that arise in mathematics and in other contexts.

Objective

Students will use fractions to figure out how much of a cookie or donut each person in a group receives.

Materials

large, soft cookies, brownies, or donuts
plastic knives
paper plates
paper napkins

Fractions become much more meaningful if they involve real-life objects, especially food! Nothing grabs students' attention more than giving four of them three donuts, or giving three of them four donuts. To continue your study of fractions, try this authentic task with students.

Have students work in groups of four. Groups can be any size you wish, depending on the fractions students are studying. Just provide one fewer or one more food item than the number of students in the group. Students must figure out a way to share the food equally. Note: Ask about any food allergies before beginning the activity.

Explain the following rules to students:

- Each student must get exactly the same amount.

- Before any food is cut, students must make a diagram to show how they will solve the problem.

- On the diagram, students must label the fractions to show how much each person will get.

- The person in charge of cutting the food must wash his or her hands first.

- Before any food is eaten, you must check their work!

Ideas for More Differentiation

Challenge more advanced students to divide 2 1/2 donuts or 3 1/3 cookies among the group.

Measuring Madness

Standards
Measurement—Apply appropriate techniques, tools, and formulas to determine measurement.

Strategy
Authentic task

Objective
Students will measure the length and width and determine the area of a basketball court, a handball court, and/or a four-square court.

Materials
rulers or yardsticks
clipboards or notebooks
sidewalk chalk

Measuring real-world objects helps math come alive for students. It also helps get the blood pumping to students' brains as they get up and move around.

1. Have students work in pairs, armed with rulers or yardsticks, clipboards, and paper.

2. Invite each pair to measure the length and width of the basketball, handball, or four-square court. Differentiate the task based on students' individual abilities. For example, pairs can measure using inches, feet, yards, or fractions of miles. They can use chalk to mark the end of a foot to help them see where to place the ruler next.

3. Back in the classroom, have students draw a diagram of the court(s) they measured and label the length and width with the units of measurement they used. Ask them to compute the area by multiplying the length times the width.

4. Invite student pairs to compare their findings with other pairs in the class. If some students find that their measurements are drastically different from others', encourage them to go outside and measure the courts again. When they come back, invite them to share where they made mistakes in their measurements.

Ideas for More Differentiation
Create a Measuring Center, where students can explore measuring items of varying size and shape. Invite them to measure using inches, feet, and yards. They can also use nonstandard units of measure, such as pretzel sticks or pencils.

Array of Buttons

Strategies
Graphic organizer

Multiple intelligences

Standard
Geometry—Use visualization, spatial reasoning, and geometric modeling to solve problems.

Objective
Students will draw circles in a chart to represent the area of a number.

Materials
Arrays of Buttons reproducible
buttons in resealable plastic bags
crayons or markers

Graphic organizers are useful thinking tools that allow students to organize information and visualize their logic. When students are working with the concept of area, it is helpful for them to practice organizing real objects into different arrays. A 3 x 4 array might represent the area of a 3" x 4" rectangle, or 12 square inches. Use this hands-on activity when introducing students to the concept of area.

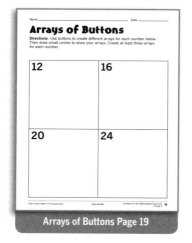

Arrays of Buttons Page 19

1. Give students a copy of the **Arrays of Buttons reproducible (page 19)** and a bag of buttons.

2. Ask them to create different arrays using the designated number of buttons. For example, in the space for number *12*, students may make a 1 x 12 array, a 3 x 4 array, or a 2 x 6 array.

3. Have students draw circles to represent the buttons. Encourage them to draw small circles in order to represent as many arrays as possible in each section of the graphic organizer.

Ideas for More Differentiation
Invite students to use their arrays to write math problems for area. Tell them each button (or circle) represents one inch or one foot. Students might write problems such as *4" x 6" = 24 square inches* or *8' x 2' = 16 square feet*.

Arrays of Buttons

Directions: Use buttons to create different arrays for each number below. Then draw small circles to show your arrays. Create at least three arrays for each number.

12	**16**
20	**24**

Soda Savvy Center

Strategies

Structured center

Cooperative group learning

Standard

Geometry—Use visualization, spatial reasoning, and geometric modeling to solve problems.

Objective

Students will design and build three-dimensional containers for three-dimensional objects.

Materials

clean, empty soda cans
tag board or cereal box cardboard
masking tape
scissors
rulers
crayons or markers

Centers are excellent tools for differentiating lessons. Even upper elementary students love to work in centers! They feel independent and enjoy moving around and performing tasks on their own. For a center to work, however, it has to be engaging enough to hold students' interest. It also should allow students to work at different levels of ability and provide several opportunities for success.

Students will probably need more than one session to complete the Soda Savvy Center project. They can work in center groups, in pairs, or individually, depending on their abilities and the available supplies.

1. Give each group, pair, or student a certain number of soda cans (the number depends on students' individual abilities).

2. Have students arrange the cans in the best array possible in order to create a carton to hold the cans. For example, you might give a pair of children 12 cans. They may decide to stack the cans in a 6 x 2 array (see illustration). Have them tape the cans together once they decide on their array.

3. When students are finished, have them measure their array's length and width and then transfer that information onto cardboard, allowing some extra room for taping space.

4. Students then tape, bend, fold, cut, and so on, to create the carton for their soda cans. This task will take ingenuity, perseverance,

and patience. Invite students to decorate their cartons and add handles or a shoulder strap using scrap materials. If possible, group students with varying skills and learning preferences. For example, put together visual/spatial, bodily/kinesthetic, logical/mathematical, and interpersonal learners. One student might figure out the best array for the container; one might construct the container; another might decorate the container; while another could skillfully direct the group's activities and keep everyone on task.

Ideas for More Differentiation

For more advanced learners, provide less concrete practice with arrays. Encourage them to extend their learning to the formula for finding area.

Extend the Activity

Invite students to work in their groups to come up with a new soda. They will give their soda a name and write a commercial advertising the product. Depending on their preferences and abilities, they can present their commercial to the class, write a print ad, or create a poster.

Probabilitease!

Strategy
Focus activity

Standard
Data Analysis and Probability—Select and use appropriate statistical methods to analyze data.

Objective
Students will analyze probability data.

Materials
paper lunch bag
index cards
marker

The following focus activity will get your students' brains in gear before you present a lesson on probability.

1. Place two index cards in a paper bag, one labeled *girls* and one labeled *boys*.

2. Tell students that you are going to draw one card from the bag ten times. Draw the first card, and have a volunteer keep track on the chalkboard using a tally chart. Replace the card, and repeat the process ten times. Depending on which card is drawn the most times, either the boys or girls will get to go to recess five minutes early or receive some other small reward.

3. Since the probability is equal, there may be a tie, so put another index card in the bag. Label this card *girls* or *boys*, whichever you wish. Don't tell students which word is on the third card.

4. As you draw cards and the tally marks add up for one group or the other, ask students to try to figure out which word you wrote on the third card.

5. Most likely, the word you wrote on the third card will be drawn more often. Lead students to understand that this happened because the ratio was two to one, or two cards to one card.

Ideas for More Differentiation
Encourage visual and tactile learners to practice rolling dice or pulling a certain color of jellybeans from a jar to practice guessing probabilities.

CHAPTER 2

Science

Hook into the Scientific Method

Standard

Science as Inquiry—Understand about scientific inquiry.

Objective

Students will use a mnemonic device to remember the steps of the scientific method.

Students enjoy science when it involves doing experiments, not just rote learning from a textbook. However, in order to understand how to investigate a problem, students must understand the scientific method, the process in which experiments are used to answer questions.

Step 1: Question

The first step is to formulate a question. Students ask themselves what they are trying to discover from the experiment. They also read and conduct research to find out what others have already learned about their question. This helps students narrow the focus of their inquiry.

Step 2: Hypothesis

The second step is to formulate the hypothesis. This means that students make an educated guess as to the outcome of their experiment. Their hypothesis must be measurable.

Step 3: Experiment

The third step is to test the hypothesis by doing an experiment. The object of the experiment is to try to confirm or disprove the hypothesis.

Step 4: Analysis

The fourth step in the process is to analyze the data. Students will evaluate what the data tells them and decide if it supports their hypothesis.

Step 5: Conclusion

The fifth step is to form a conclusion. To conclude the inquiry, students must use the results of their experiment to reject or confirm the hypothesis.

The five steps of the scientific method can be difficult for students to remember. Use the following rehearsal activity to create a mnemonic that helps students remember the steps.

Steps of the Scientific Method

Question
Hypothesis
Experiment
Analysis
Conclusion

Have students use the Think-Pair-Share method to come up with clever, easy-to-remember mnemonic devices. First, have each student think individually about words and phrases that could represent the five steps of the scientific method. Then have students work with partners to brainstorm a mnemonic device they will present to the class. Invite the class to vote on which device is the most imaginative, easiest to remember, and so on. Some examples include:

Quick **H**orses **E**at **A**pples **C**arelessly!

Quit **H**aving **E**arly **A**rt **C**lass!

Queen **H**eather **E**ats **A**pple **C**ake!

Quick, **H**enry, **E**arn **A**nother **C**andy!

Opposites Attract

Standard
Physical Science—Understand light, heat, electricity, and magnetism.

Objective
Students will pretend to be magnetic poles searching for their polar opposites.

Strategies
Multiple intelligences

Role play

Materials
rulers
index cards (one for each student)
tape or safety pins
song "Opposites Attract" by Paula Abdul (on CD or audiotape)
CD or tape player

How many times do you hear students singing or humming jingles or popular songs? Music can make learning and remembering concepts easier. Connect to students' musical intelligence when introducing the concept that polar opposites of magnets attract by using the first verse and chorus of Paula Abdul's song "Opposites Attract."

1. Before the activity, use a marker to write *N* on half of the index cards and *S* on the other half. Give half of the students an *N* card and the other half an *S* card. Have students tape or pin the cards to their shirts.

2. Give each "N student" two rulers, one for each hand. Prepare a "student magnet" by pairing an N student with an "S student" (the N student extends the ruler in his or her left hand to the S student).

3. Play the first verse and chorus of the song. (Use the first verse and chorus only, as the second verse may not be appropriate.) While the music plays, N–S magnets walk around as a unit, looking for their opposites. For example, an N student extends a ruler to an S student. If an N student approaches another N student, or an S student approaches another S student, they shout *Repel!* and back away. The object of the game is to connect all the "magnets" by the time the music ends.

Various Voices

Standard

Physical Science—Understand properties of objects and materials.

Objective

Students will practice definitions of core vocabulary.

Learning definitions of core vocabulary can be challenging, but also fun if it's approached in the right way! Tap into your students' linguistic, musical, and interpersonal intelligences by inviting them to use their voices when studying vocabulary.

For example, perhaps students are studying electromagnets. On chart paper, write the definition for an electromagnet: *Electromagnet—A temporary magnet made by passing current through wire that is wrapped around an iron core.*

To simply read this definition aloud is boring and ineffective. Ask several volunteers to come to the front of the room. Each student reads the definition using a different voice and appropriate actions and movements. For example, a student can read like a robot while making robotic movements. Students will have blast! Try these different voices with corresponding motions. Ask students to help add voices to this list:

Dude, it's like a totally awesome temporary magnet!

- robot
- alien (Martian)
- surfer dude
- baby
- vampire
- queen
- lamb

For example, the "surfer dude" could have a conversation with the "vampire." The vampire could say that he doesn't understand what an electromagnet is, and the surfer dude could explain it.

Ideas for More Differentiation

Invite your musical learners to write a song or rap about the core vocabulary using the voice and style of one of these characters. Students can work with partners to perform for the class.

Circuit Raps

Standard

Physical Science—Understand light, heat, electricity, and magnetism.

Objective

Students will write a rap that explains circuitry.

Strategies

Rehearsal

Rhyme/rap

Performance

When students are investigating series and parallel circuits, they should use batteries, light bulbs, and wire in order to make real connections. That is the fun part of science—using real materials to do authentic, hands-on projects. However, when it comes time to get ready for the test, how can students study? They can write a rap!

Invite students to access their musical and linguistic abilities to compare the different kinds of circuits. After they write and practice their raps, they can perform them for the class.

Have students review what they know about closed circuits and parallel circuits and draw pictures to illustrate the flow of electricity in each circuit. As they read and draw, encourage them to start thinking about their rap. Have them refer to explanations of the circuits in their science texts while writing. Before students begin, you may want to play a child-appropriate rap for students as an example.

Raps often repeat certain words or phrases. They also integrate a rhythmic beat with the words.

Example:

A parallel path has more than one,

More than one path for the current to travel.

Remove one bulb and the current still moves

Down the other path, down the other path.

The other bulb stays lit, it stays lit.

It's still light. No night.

There is one path,

I said one path,

For the current in a series circuit.

Remove one bulb,

And the path is broken.

I said broken, just broken.

No bulb on the circuit will light.

Now it's dark,

Just dark.

Racing to Learn

Strategies
Metaphor/analogy

Multiple intelligences

Standard
Physical Sciences—Understand light, heat, electricity, and magnetism.

Objective
Students will use metaphor to enhance their understanding of electricity.

Materials
Indy 500 Goes Electric reproducible

Accessing prior knowledge is helpful when learning new concepts. It helps students connect new learning to something they already know. The use of metaphor is an effective tool to create those connections in students' minds.

The concepts of circuitry and electricity can be challenging at first. Connect to students' prior knowledge by using this common metaphor—a racetrack. Explain the following racetrack metaphor to students, emphasizing appropriate core vocabulary: *circuit, electric current, conductor, switch, insulator, resistor,* and *electric cell.* Encourage students to visualize the metaphor as you read it aloud. This will be especially helpful to your verbal/linguistic learners. Tell students:

The Indianapolis 500 takes place on a large, oval track. One revolution around the track is called a circuit. Cars race around the track, just as electric current moves around a circuit of wire. The asphalt of the track acts as the conductor for cars, just as the wire acts as the conductor of electricity.

If a car crashes, all the cars behind it are forced to stop. In an electrical circuit, a switch is used to disconnect the wire and force the current to stop flowing.

On the racetrack, cars must periodically pull in for pit stops when signaled by the flagman. In an electrical circuit, a switch can also be used to send electricity to another destination.

Also on the racetrack, there are bumpers along the sides of the track to insulate, or protect, people from cars that crash. On the outside of wire, there is material that insulates the electrical current from causing an accident, called an insulator.

When there is a hazard on a racetrack, cones are placed around it to reduce the number of lanes until the hazard is cleared. This causes several lanes of traffic to be reduced down to one. In an electrical circuit, a resistor works in much the same way. It limits the current that can flow through the circuit.

The engine in a racecar provides the power for movement. An electric current is stored in an electric cell, or battery, which powers electrical devices.

To help visual learners, who may make up most of your classroom, distribute a copy of the **Indy 500 Goes Electric reproducible (page 30)**. This sheet provides a visual comparison of each component in the racetrack metaphor.

Ideas for More Differentiation

Invite more advanced students to compact their learning by creating an additional metaphor for an electrical circuit. Invite them to illustrate their comparisons on a bulletin board for the class.

▶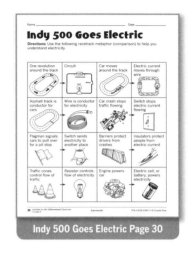

Indy 500 Goes Electric Page 30

Name _____ Date _____

Indy 500 Goes Electric

Directions: Use the following racetrack metaphor (comparison) to help you understand electricity.

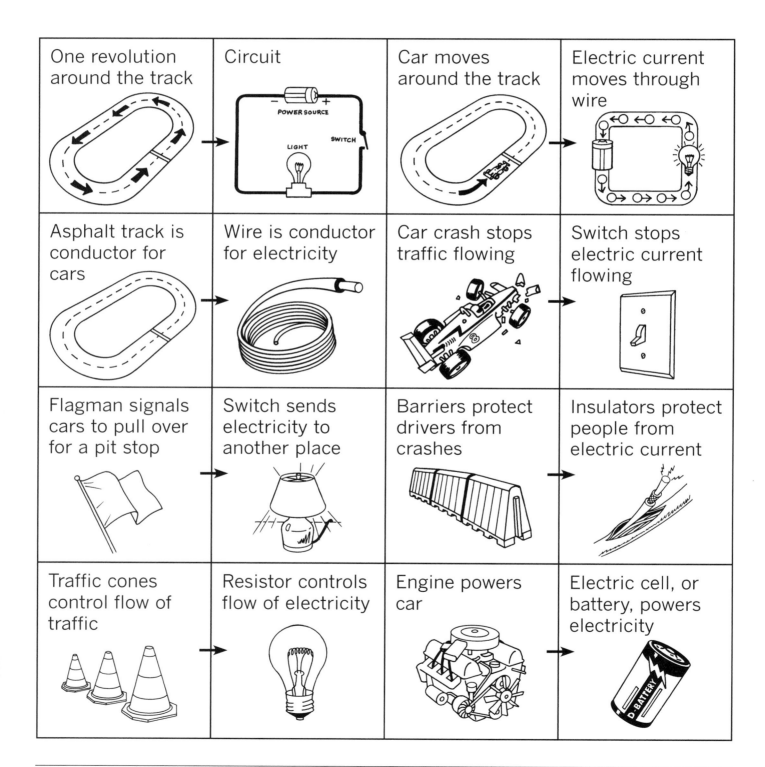

Cover Up!

Standard
Life Science—Understand characteristics of organisms.
Understand organisms and environments.

Objective
Students will examine animal coverings and associate them with an animal's need to adapt to its environment.

Materials
Animal Expert reproducible
snake skins (available at pet stores)
realistic plastic fish with scales
swatches of synthetic fur
seashells of various shapes and sizes
bird feathers (available at art supply stores)
magnifying glasses
plastic storage containers
nonfiction books and other resources about animals
drawing paper
colored pencils or crayons

Strategies
Graphic organizer

Exploratory center

Gain students' attention by asking them if their parents have ever chased them out the door with a coat calling: *You forgot your coat! You'll freeze to death out there!* Explain that humans do not have special adaptations to protect them from the elements, as animals do. Although mammals, such as humans, are warm-blooded, we still need to wear coats in order to stay warm on cold days.

To help students explore animal adaptations, create an Animal Coverings Center. Display the animal covering materials (see materials list) in separate plastic storage containers. Place nonfiction animal books, encyclopedias, magnifying glasses, drawing paper, and colored pencils or crayons in the center as well.

Allow students to explore each item using the magnifying glasses. Then have them fold a piece of drawing paper into four sections. In each section, have them draw what they see under the magnifying glass for each animal covering. Then ask students to name and describe the covering, and how it helps the animal survive. Allow them to do additional research in books and on the Internet before reporting their findings.

For example:

- *Fur keeps animals warm. It is often colored to blend in with the animal's environment for the purpose of camouflage.*

- *Feathers help birds stay warm and dry. They are lightweight, which allows birds to fly.*

- *A fish's scales help protect the fish from other animals and from diseases.*

- *A reptile's scales help protect the reptile from injury and from drying out. A snake's scales form a smooth covering, which helps it move along the ground.*

- *A snail's shell protects its soft body.*

Students can also focus on one particular animal. Invite students to choose one animal and focus on how its parts (e.g., teeth, claws, ears, eyes, tail) and covering (e.g., fur, scales, feathers) help it to survive in its environment. Have plenty of **Animal Expert reproducibles (page 33)** available in the center to help students record and organize animal facts.

Encourage students to add to the collection of animal coverings in the center. They can bring in the body of an insect, such as a sow bug, cricket, or butterfly. Or, perhaps they have a pet they would like to bring in for classmates to observe.

Ideas for More Differentiation

Have students form center groups in which they can "jigsaw" tasks. Ask each group member to research one animal covering (fur, feathers, scales, shell, skin) and then come back together to report their findings.

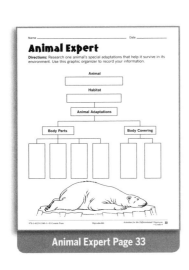

Animal Expert Page 33

ANIMAL COVERING CENTER

Animal Expert

Directions: Research one animal's special adaptations that help it survive in its environment. Use this graphic organizer to record your information.

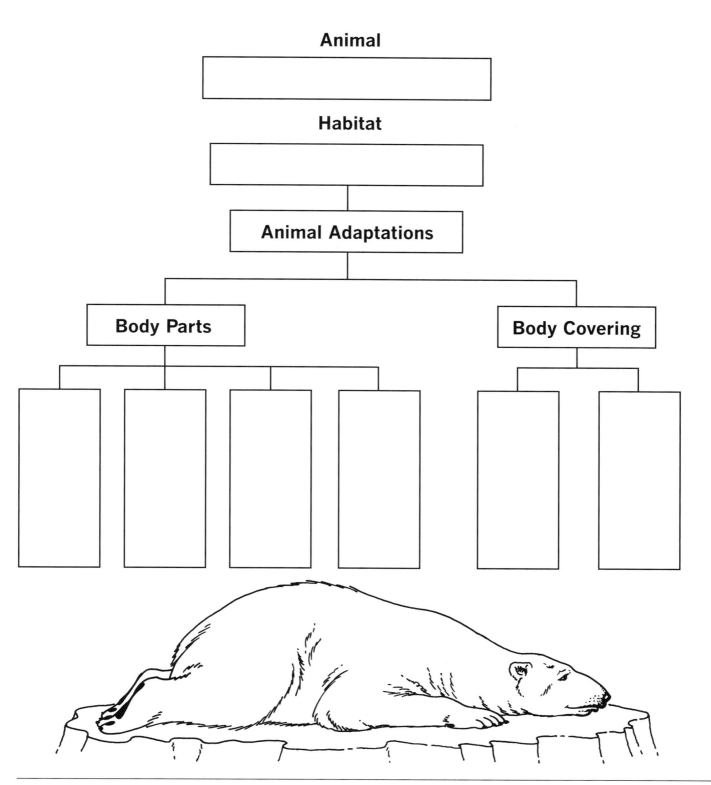

Animal

Habitat

Animal Adaptations

Body Parts   **Body Covering**

Biomes Rotation Reflection

Strategies

Rotation reflection

Cooperative group learning

Standard
Life Science—Understand organisms and environments.

Objective
Students will reflect on what they learn about biomes.

Materials
6 large pieces of chart paper
6 broad-tipped markers of different colors
masking tape

The rotation reflection strategy is very effective for reviewing material already learned. For this activity, students work in six cooperative groups to review and discuss information posted on charts around the classroom.

1. Label separate pieces of chart paper with the names of the six biomes: *Tropical Rain Forest, Grassland, Deciduous Forest, Desert, Taiga,* and *Tundra.* Post the charts around the classroom low enough for students to easily see and reach.

2. Divide the class into six groups. Give each group a marker of a different color in order to keep track of what they write.

3. Decide on a time limit for each biome. Give the signal for students to start.

4. Have each group go to a chart. Invite them to brainstorm as much about that biome as they can while one student writes their ideas on the chart.

5. After the time is up, signal for groups to move to the next biome. Continue until all groups have visited each biome.

6. When the rotation is complete, invite groups to share information from their last chart. During this review, the class can determine if any information is incorrect or missing.

Ideas for More Differentiation
Use the cubing strategy to engage student groups in further investigation of each biome. Label the cube with tasks at different skill levels from which students can choose. For example: *Use a Venn diagram to compare your biome to another; design a biome diorama; research which animals are endangered in your biome; create a mural of your biome;* and so on.

People and the Environment

Standard
Science in Personal and Social Perspectives—Understand changes in environments.

Strategies
Choice board

Journaling

Objective
Students will choose a project to discover how people have changed an ecosystem.

Materials
Ecosystem Choice Board reproducible

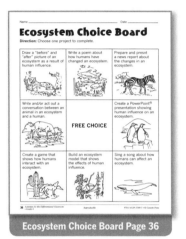

Ecosystem Choice Board Page 36

Choice Boards give students a choice of activities to show what they've learned. These flexible projects allow students to work at their own readiness levels. In order to support all students, provide materials and books at different reading levels and several activity choices.

In fourth grade, students learn about ecosystems and how humans change their environments in either beneficial, neutral, or detrimental ways. Give students a copy of the **Ecosystem Choice Board reproducible (page 36)**. Have students select one of the projects to show what they've learned about humans' effect on ecosystems. Students may work alone or with a partner.

To close the activity, give students a chance to share their work with the class. Then encourage them to reflect on their learning in their journals.

Ecosystem Choice Board

Direction: Choose one project to complete.

Draw a "before" and "after" picture of an ecosystem as a result of human influence. 	Write a poem about how humans have changed an ecosystem. 	Prepare and presnt a news report about the changes in an ecosystem. 
Write and/or act out a conversation between an animal in an ecosystem and a human. 	**FREE CHOICE**	Create a PowerPoint® presentation showing human influence on an ecosystem. 
Create a game that shows how humans interact with an ecosystem. 	Build an ecosystem model that shows the effects of human influence. 	Sing a song about how humans can affect an ecosystem. 

Rock Walk

Standard
Earth and Space Science—Understand properties of earth materials.

Strategy
Rehearsal

Objective
Students will play a game to match vocabulary words and definitions.

Materials
sentence strips
marker
scissors
pocket chart
fun "rock" music
CD or cassette player

After learning about different types of rocks, invite students to play "The Rock Walk."

1. Before playing the game, write rock names and their definitions on separate sentence strips. Cut apart the strips as needed. For example, write *magma* on one strip, and its definition, *melted rock that stays below the earth's surface,* on another.

2. To play the game, give half the class vocabulary word strips. Give the other half the definitions to those words. The goal is for students to find their partner, pairing up words with the correct definitions. While students are searching, play some fun "rock" music to inspire students to move, such as "We Will Rock You" by Queen, "Rock Around the Clock" by Bill Haley and His Comets, or "Old Time Rock and Roll" by Bob Seger.

3. Encourage students to mingle around the room, reading definitions and rock names until they match each rock to its definition.

4. After two students have found their word/definition match, they place their sentence strips in a pocket chart at the front of the room. They can then help their classmates find word/definition matches.

Ideas for More Differentiation
Have students make word webs for assigned rocks. Have them write the rock name and glue a picture in the center circle and write details in the outer circles. For example: *obsidian—formed from lava contacting water; found around volcanoes; looks like black glass; semiprecious stone.*

Mad for Scientists

Standard

History and Nature of Science—Understand science as a human endeavor.

Objective

Students will conduct research to learn about a scientist and present their information to the class.

Materials

Mad for Scientists reproducible
resources about scientists and scientific discoveries
Internet access

It's important that students understand the reason we have all the technological and medical advances in the world today. They are the result of the hard work of scientists.

Invite student pairs to choose and research a scientist for a class presentation. Tell them to choose a scientist based on their interest in what he or she discovered or contributed to the world of science. Provide a wide range of resources from which students can do their research. Appeal to different readiness levels by including hi-low books, biographies at different grade levels, encyclopedias, and a list of appropriate Web sites available on the Internet.

For a great resource on science biographies written at children's level, go to the Amazon.com Web site, and search using key words

science and *children's books*. There are also many interesting Web sites available on the Internet (search using key words *famous scientists*). You might also try kid-centered search engines such as *Yahooligans.com, Askforkids.com,* and *Kidsclick.org.*

See the list of names on page 39 for some famous scientists students may want to research.

Famous Scientists

Aglaonika (female Greek astronomer; predicted times and locations of lunar eclipses)

Archimedes (discovered *pi*; one of history's greatest mathematicians)

Aristotle (studied anatomy, astronomy, embryology, geography, geology, meteorology, physics, and zoology)

Nicholas Copernicus (hypothesized that planets revolve around the sun)

Marie Curie (physicist famous for her work on radioactivity)

Charles Darwin (documented theory of evolution)

Leonard da Vinci (mechanical inventor and artist)

Thomas Edison (introduced the modern use of electricity)

Albert Einstein (theory of relativity)

Benjamin Franklin (investigated electricity; invented many terms still used today, e.g., *positive, negative, battery, conductor*)

Galileo Galilei (developed scientific method; improved the telescope)

Sybil Masters (first U.S. female inventor; invented a way to preserve Indian corn for the colonists)

Isaac Newton (laws of motion)

Wilhelm Conrad Rontgen (discovered X-rays)

Carl Sagan (popularized science)

Nikola Tesla (invented alternating current transmission systems)

Trotula of Solerno (taught male doctors about childbirth)

Have students use the **Mad for Scientists graphic organizer (page 40)** to organize their information for the presentation. Encourage students to make their presentations more exciting and interesting by dressing up as the scientist and using visuals such as pictures, drawings, charts, and props. Students can role-play, write a script or short play, or present factual information as a news report.

Mad for Scientists Page 40

Name _____ Date _____

Mad for Scientists

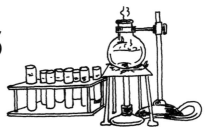

Directions: Use this chart to help you organize information about your scientist.

Who is your scientist?

Where was the most important work done?

When was the important work done?

What was his/her most important work?

What else did this scientist contribute?

Why was the work done? Why was it important?

How is this scientist's work important to my life?

Fast Five Facts

Standard
History and Nature of Science—Understand science as a human endeavor.

Strategies
Sponge activity
After-learning assessment

Objective
Students will earn points by answering questions about scientists.

Materials
completed Mad for Scientists graphic organizers (see page 40)

Do you ever have an extra few minutes right before recess or before class lets out for the day? You probably glance at the clock and think: *What can I do to make the most of these five minutes?* Use this motivating sponge activity to soak up those extra minutes!

This simple game takes no prep time because students already did the work on their graphic organizers. It is a great review of the information students presented in their reports. You'll be able to tell who learned the information and listened carefully to the presentations.

After students present their scientist reports, collect their completed graphic organizers. Use these organizers to quiz students on what they've just learned in class. Divide the class into two teams, for example, Team Einstein and Team Newton. Challenge students to answer five questions pulled from the graphic organizers. For example:

- *Which scientist invented X-rays?*

- *Where was Marie Curie born?*

- *How did Galileo improve the telescope?*

- *How did Copernicus change our view of the universe?*

- *How did Benjamin Franklin contribute to the development of electricity?*

When a team answers correctly, award them one point. Or, you might decide not to form teams at all, but just toss out a question and toss back a reward for the right answer, such as a piece of candy or a new pencil eraser!

Social Studies

Go to the Source

Standard
Understand individual development and identity.

Objective
Students will interview family members or friends to learn about primary sources and how views of historical events can differ.

Materials
Interview Questions reproducible

When studying history, students should understand the importance of primary source information. A primary source is a person who witnessed an event firsthand or was part of an historical event. The most common primary sources are journals, letters, and sometimes newspapers. Emphasize to students that individual views of the same event can differ depending on who is viewing it or telling about it.

Students can practice gathering primary-source information by interviewing friends or family members. For example, Leah can interview her brother about a basketball game in which he played. She can then interview her mother, who was a spectator at the event. Leah will then compare the interviews to see how two perspectives of the same event might overlap and differ.

Be sensitive to privacy issues when asking students to interview family members. Some families are very private and are uncomfortable sharing information. That's okay! Instead of a family member, students can interview two friends who experienced the same event, such as a sports game, field trip, circus, or thunderstorm.

◄ Invite students to use the **Interview Questions reproducible (page 43)** to help them gather information during their interviews. To make this reproducible even more effective, make double-sided copies so students can use one side for each interview.

Interview Questions Page 43

Name _____ Date _____

Interview Questions

Directions: Use the following questions to interview your subject.

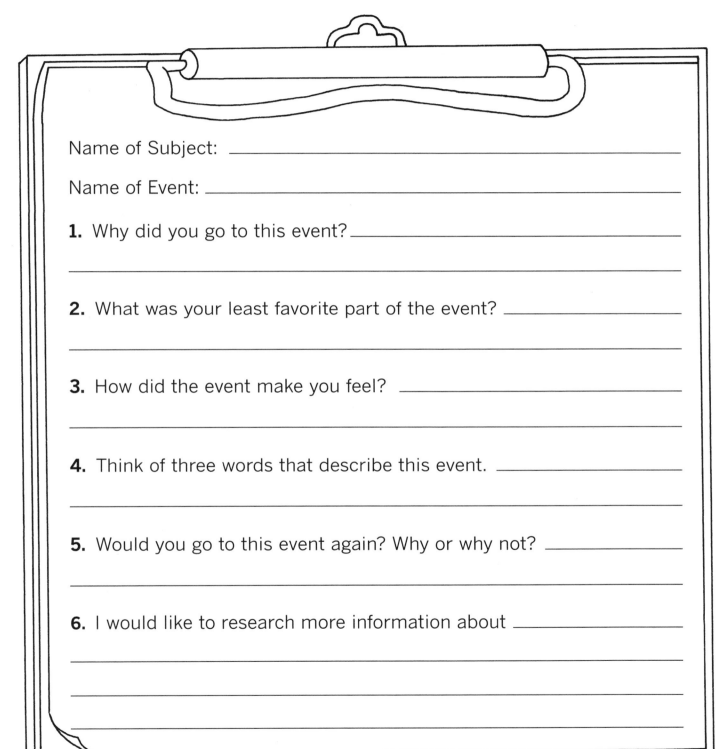

Name of Subject: _____

Name of Event: _____

1. Why did you go to this event? _____

_____

2. What was your least favorite part of the event? _____

_____

3. How did the event make you feel? _____

_____

4. Think of three words that describe this event. _____

_____

5. Would you go to this event again? Why or why not? _____

_____

6. I would like to research more information about _____

_____

_____

The Wedding Cake

Strategy
Graphic organizer

Standard
The standard will depend on the concepts students are currently studying.

Objective
Students will use a graphic organizer to learn causeeffect relationships between events.

Cause–effect relationships are especially important in the study of history. One great strategy for helping students understand cause–effect relationships is the "wedding cake" graphic organizer. Use this graphic organizer on an overhead or the chalkboard to explain connecting information or events.

Preface the lesson by explaining that in history, one thing leads to, or causes, another. For every action (cause), there is a reaction (effect). For example, in the study of the California gold rush, you might use the wedding cake organizer as follows:

Marshall discovered gold in 1848.

Newspapers and word of mouth spread news of gold. Gold fever struck!

By 1849 people from around the world came to California to make their fortunes. These people were called *forty-niners*.

California's population changed as a result of this new rush of migrants. Small towns quickly grew into large cities, such as San Francisco. In 1848 there were about 900 people in the town. By 1850 the city's population reached 35,000.

Industry in California developed rapidly. Homes had to be built for all newcomers. Hotels, stores, restaurants, and laundries were built. People made fortunes by charging high prices for scarce goods. Entrepreneurs discovered new ways to meet consumer needs (e.g., Levi Straus used metal rivets in blue jeans to make them stronger for miners).

California's population changed as a result of the new rush of immigrants.

Different cultures, languages, customs, races, and religions abounded in California.

Many migrants (Mexicans, African-Americans, Chinese) faced discrimination and were forced off the mining camps or not paid for their services. Native Americans were forced off their land when gold was found or died from diseases brought by the migrants.

Small towns quickly grew into large cities.

Crime grew rapidly. Dozens of violent crimes were committed each day.

People wanted justice. Some took the law into their own hands and became vigilantes. In San Francisco, the Committee of Vigilance formed. This committee was made up of 180 citizens who would arrest, try, and punish criminals.

Challenge your students to create their own "wedding cakes" using the **Wedding Cake Graphic Organizer (page 46)**. Give them the first layer, and then let them go! You could also allow students to make wedding cakes on squares of colorful construction paper, complete with decorations and illustrations.

▶

Wedding Cake Page 46

Wedding Cake

Directions: Use this organizer to show how one event connects to the next.

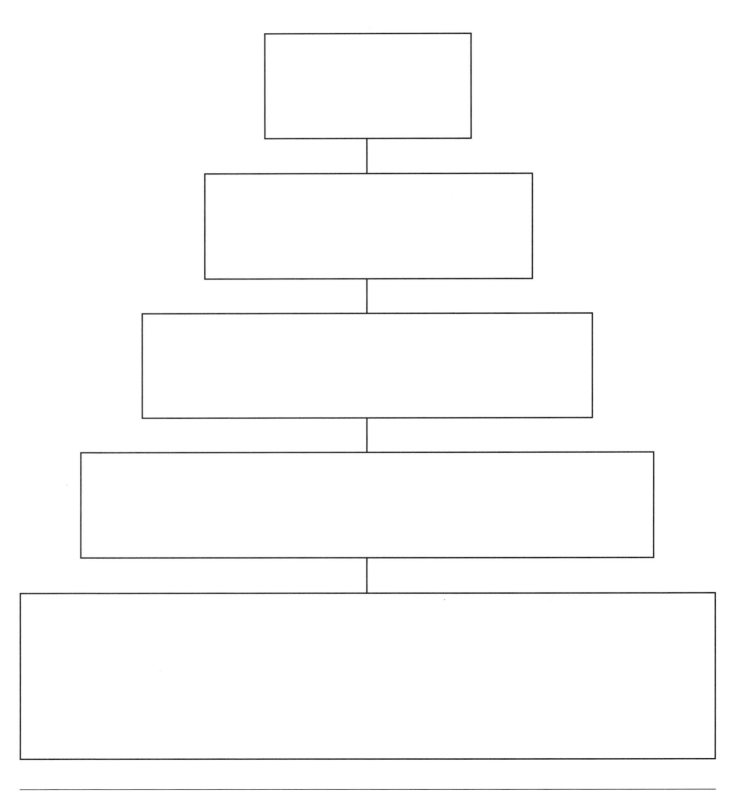

Reproducible

978-1-4129-5340-5 • © Corwin Press

State Debate

Standard

Understand the ways human beings view themselves in and over time.
Understand interactions among individuals, groups, and institutions.
Understand interactions among people, places, and environments.

Objective

Students will state an opinion about historical events and use facts to support their opinion.

The state in which students live has gone through many changes over time. After students have learned about their changing state, offer them a new challenge. Invite students to choose the event or person they think changed their state the most.

1. Give students a copy of the **State Debate graphic organizer (page 48)**. They can use this sheet to organize information about their chosen event or person. Allow students time to do additional research.

2. When students are done with their research, invite them to participate in a debate. You or another student can act as a moderator while students share their opinions with the class. Invite two students at a time to the front of the class. One student presents his or her opinion and supporting evidence, then the next student has a chance to speak. Students' opinions must be based on facts from textbooks or other sources.

3. One student can then challenge the other student's opinion. For example: *I disagree that the missionaries changed California the most because the population of California did not change as much as it did during the Gold Rush.* Then give the other student an opportunity to defend his or her position.

4. Invite students to vote on which opinion was the most convincing and why.

5. Invite students to reflect on this experience in their journals. They can write a short summary of their research or write more opinions about the class debate.

State Debate Page 48

Name _____ Date _____

State Debate

Directions: You studied how your state has changed over time. Choose one event or person who you think changed your state the most. Use this graphic organizer to help you prepare for a class debate.

What event or person changed your state the most?

List facts about your state before the event or the person changed it.	List facts about your state after the event or the person changed it.

978-1-4129-5340-5 • © Corwin Press

Our State Is Great!

Standard

Understand how people organize for the production, distribution, and consumption of goods and services.

Objective

Students will create an advertisement (poster, newspaper ad, or live-action commercial) to encourage people to visit their state.

Every state has its unique natural wonders and attractions. With students, discuss what special attractions bring tourists to your state. For example, Arizona is known for the Grand Canyon and various Native American ruins; California is known for Hollywood, Disneyland, and Napa Valley; and Louisiana is known for the Mississippi River, New Orleans, and Mardi Gras.

Have students work in pairs to think about how they could advertise their state's unique qualities and attractions to tourists. Encourage them to think about human-made attractions (amusement parks, libraries, museums) as well as natural wonders (mountain rangers, deserts, forests, oceans, lakes).

Verbal/linguistic and visual/spatial learners might enjoy creating a poster, travel brochure, or magazine ad that advertises their home state. Kinesthetic and interpersonal learners might enjoy creating a commercial or song to perform for the class.

Display books about your state, and visit a travel agency to gather brochures, books, and other materials students can use. In addition, ask students to bring in newspaper and magazine ads for various products and places. Put all the materials at an Our State Is Great! Center.

In the center, display the **Our State Choice Wheel (page 50)** from which students can choose how to present their advertisements.

When students finish their chosen assignments, have an Our Great State Day in your classroom! Invite other classes to explore students' travel brochures, print ads, and posters. Then ask pairs to perform their songs and commercials for your visitors.

▶

Strategies

Choice board

Center

Multiple intelligences

Our State Choice Wheel Page 50

Our State Choice Wheel

Directions: Choose one project to complete.

 978-1-4129-5340-5 • © *Corwin Press*

Oh Say, Can You Rewrite This, Please?

Standard

Understand the ideals, principles, and practices of citizenship in a democratic republic.

Objective

Students will rewrite "The Star-Spangled Banner" in their own words.

This musical focus activity will help grab students' attention before your next social studies lesson on American history and citizenship. Write this on the board or overhead:

Hey, can you see, when the sun rises,
The same thing we proudly saluted when the sun set last night?

Invite a volunteer to read the text aloud, and then guess what it is. Guide students to see that it is the first line of "The Star-Spangled Banner" written in twenty-first century English.

Place students into groups of three, and challenge them to rewrite the rest of the anthem. This should lead into a wonderful discussion on the meaning of "The Star-Spangled Banner" and how and why it was written. Give students the basic facts: *Francis Scott Key wrote the song in 1814 during the War of 1812. The actual "star-spangled banner," or flag, was 30' x 42', the largest battle flag ever flown!*

Examples:

Hey, can you see, when the sun rises,
The same thing we proudly saluted when the sun set last night?
Whose wide stripes and bright stars, during the dangerous battle,
We saw over the fortress walls, were bravely waving in the wind?
Red light shone from rockets, bombs exploded in midair,
Showing us that our flag was still in one piece.
Hey, does that star-covered flag still wave
Over the land of the free and the home of the brave?
Look! Now that it's morning, we can see that our flag was not destroyed!
During the battle last night, we looked over the fort walls—guess whose wide stripes and bright stars were still waving in the breeze?
The rockets and bombs flying through the air gave off enough light for us to see that the flag was still in one piece.
Hey, is our star-covered flag still waving over America, the land of the free and the home of the brave?
You bet it is!

State Acrostics

Strategy
Multiple intelligences

Standard
Understand the ideals, principles, and practices of citizenship in a democratic republic.

Objective
Students will write an acrostic poem that describes their relationship with the state.

Materials
calligraphy markers
construction paper or other publishing paper

As students learn about their state, make sure they are making personal connections so they feel a sense of pride and ownership. Students should realize that they are the next generation of voters, the next generation of decision-makers, without whom a democracy cannot flourish.

Invite students to combine what they've learned about their state with their own feelings or experiences. Have them write an acrostic poem that describes what they've learned and how they connect to their state.

1. To begin, explain to students that an acrostic poem uses each letter in a word to start each line of the poem. In this case, the subject of the poem and the word on which it is based is the name of your state.

2. Have students write the state name vertically down the side of a piece of paper. Then instruct them to write a word, phrase, or sentence that begins with each letter in the state's name. (Demonstrate by using the following examples for Louisiana and California.)

3. When students are ready to publish their poems, they can use a calligraphy marker to make the first letter of each line stand out. Encourage them to decorate their poems with illustrations and pictures and then glue their papers to colorful construction paper.

Following are two of examples for the states of Louisiana and California:

Labor of love

Ocean so near

Unusal weather

I've lived here forever

So sad to leave

I'll miss my friends

Angry at Katrina

New Orleans, come back

Always hope

City of Angels

Always sunny

Land for farming

Islands off the shore

Fine, warm weather

Open, sandy beaches

Race for gold!

Newcomers abound

In history of missions

A place for me

Go, Pony Express!

Standard

Understand how people organize for the production, distribution, and consumption of goods and services.

Objective

Students will create and run a relay race to reenact the Pony Express.

Materials

"station markers" such as cones, Frisbees, beanbags (one per student)
2 "cantinas" (e.g., backpacks)

Bring the story of the Pony Express to life by engaging students in the following role-play. This exciting activity is especially appealing to students with interpersonal and kinesthetic intelligences.

1. Begin by telling students the story of the Pony Express: *In 1860, there was a growing need to get mail from one end of the United States to the other. A man named William H. Russell had an idea.*

A team of horseback riders would race with the mail from the state of Missouri to the state of California. Riders would change horses at stations every 10 to 15 miles along the route. After about 100 miles, one rider would give the mail (carried in leather boxes called cantinas) to a fresh rider. The exhausted rider rested and then took mail back the way he came.

2. Invite children to role-play being part of the Pony Express. Outside on the playground, set up cones, beanbags, Frisbees, or other markers in two rows. The markers in each row should be about 40 feet apart. The rows should be about 20 feet apart.

3. Divide the class into two teams, and assign each team to one of the rows. Have each team member stand by a marker.

4. Give the two students at the beginning markers the cantinas. When you give the signal, they race to the next marker and hand their cantinas to the next rider. This rider runs to the next marker, handing off the cantina to the next rider down the row, and so on.

5. Have students continue running to markers and handing off the cantina until they reach the last marker. The last rider then runs back to the student who gave him or her the cantina, and the race moves in reverse.

6. The team whose rider reaches the beginning marker first wins.

Ideas for More Differentiation

Encourage students to come up with metaphors or analogies that compare the Pony Express to common things such as a relay race or modern-day delivery services such as UPS or Federal Express.

Democracy in Action

Standard

Understand how people create and change structures of power, authority, and governance.

Objective

Students will use role-play to enact a city council meeting.

Students can gain real understanding of the powers of democracy through role play. To help students understand how a democracy works, enact a mock city council meeting.

1. Begin by initiating a class discussion about common city problems, such as litter in beaches and parks, broken traffic signals, substandard playground equipment and public restrooms at parks, unrepaired potholes, underfunded animal shelters, and more.

2. With students, agree on the cost for each of item. For example, buying trashcans for the beaches might cost $100. Write the cost of each item on chart paper. After dollar amounts are allotted for each item, come up with a total city budget (e.g., $1,000).

3. Choose a student to be mayor (or ask the class to elect one), and then choose or elect a few more volunteers to act as city council members.

4. Invite your mayor to the front of the room to run the meeting. Give him or her a gavel (e.g., ruler). The "city council" also sits at the front, alongside the mayor. The rest of class, as community members, will request the items they most want for the city.

5. Tell students to begin the meeting. Community members will take turns standing and speaking to the council. Speakers must provide reasons for the items or services they want.

6. The city council must decide on which items or services it will spend money until the $1,000 is gone. Have the mayor and the city council go outside or to a private area of the room to make their decisions.

7. Finally, the city council will present its decisions to your classroom community. Follow up with a discussion about democracy in action. Allow students to debate the issues.

Freedom of Expression

Standards

Understand interactions among individuals, groups, and institutions.
Understand the ways human beings view themselves in and over time.

Strategies
Exploratory center

Multiple intelligences

Objective

Students will explore different songs that were written in response to historical events.

In the study of history, students must learn the relationships between historical events and the people affected by those events. Understanding this cause–effect relationship is essential for learning about the past as well as planning for the future.

Music is a great way to bring history alive in your classroom. You can use music in a variety of ways, letting the lyrics help tell the stories of historical events.

For example, explain to students that in the 1930s during the Great Depression, the southern part of the central United States suffered horribly from windstorms. The effects, known as the Dust Bowl, the loss of homes and livelihoods, were described by singer/songwriter Woody Guthrie. A few of his song titles about the Dust Bowl include "Dust Bowl Blues," "Dust Bowl Refugees," and "The Great Dust Storm."

If possible, allow students to listen to Woody Guthrie songs as part of learning about the Dust Bowl.

Set up an exploratory Musical History Center in your classroom that appeals to students' various intelligences (musical/rhythmic, visual/ spatial, bodily/kinesthetic, intrapersonal, and interpersonal). Invite students to explore and respond to different kinds of music about places or historical events. Provide a variety of supplies that students can use to express their ideas about the music.

For example:

- Provide lyrics and recordings of various state songs. Students can listen with headphones and discover how the lyrics relate to each state. (Make sure to include songs about your own state, as well.)

- Students can research singers and songwriters who were born in their home state by doing an Internet search. Have them search using the key words *famous musicians* (or *singers*) *from* (*their state's name*). With your diligent supervision, students can learn about the musicians and songs they wrote to see how they connect to real events. For example, Billy Joel wrote about the hardships caused by factory shutdowns in Allentown, Pennsylvania, in his song "Allentown."

- Challenge students to write their own lyrics about a past or current historical event occurring in your city, state, or the world at large. Invite them to write lyrics that tell about the event, how they feel about the event, or how the event has affected people. Your musical students may even be able to set their lyrics to music.

Ideas for More Differentiation

- Invite students to create a dance or act out an event described in the lyrics of a song.

- Others may want to respond to music by creating a poster or painting a picture to express what they've learned.

I Am

Standards

Understand culture and cultural diversity.
Understand individual development and identity.

Strategy
Multiple intelligences

Objective

Students will write a poem to tell about themselves.

Each student needs to feel that he or she belongs in the community. Differences between students should be celebrated, and similarities should be embraced. To help students celebrate themselves, invite them to write "I Am" poems. This poem is very simple. The first two words of each line are *I am*. Students will write short phrases or sentences that describe who they are. Allow students to express themselves in any way they wish. The can choose serious ideas, silly ideas, personal and family ideas, or simple facts. For example:

Alicia	Eric
I am a Californian.	I am my mother's son.
I am brave.	I am an only child.
I am Hispanic.	I am good at math.
I am a good dancer.	I am a citizen of the United States.
I am an American.	I am funny.
I am generous.	I am a soccer player.
I am intelligent.	I am going to be president of this country.
I am a great friend.	I am a loyal friend.
I am proud to be me.	I am going to make this world a better place.

This simple format makes it easy for every student to be successful. Perhaps students will want to publish their poems in a class book or display them on a bulletin board. (Get students' permission before displaying poems, as poems might be very private.)

Ideas for More Differentiation

Collect poems from students who feel comfortable sharing them. Read each poem aloud without revealing the name. Invite the class to guess who is being described in each poem. After each poem is read, ask students to share other words or ideas that might describe that student.

Language Arts

"1, 3, 2"

Standard

Apply a wide range of strategies to comprehend, interpret, evaluate, and appreciate texts. Draw on prior experience, interactions with other readers and writers, knowledge of word meaning and of other texts, word identification strategies, and understanding of textural features.

Objective

Students will use a graphic organizer to help them analyze the structure of a story.

Materials

Easy as 1, 3, 2! reproducible

Writing to retell a story is difficult for many students. Some students provide so much detail that they could write for hours and still not finish, while others have difficulty just getting started.

Students can often identify the beginning and ending of a story but have difficulty recognizing where the middle of the story begins and ends. This is where the "1, 3, 2" approach is useful. This strategy get students to: 1) retell the first part of the story, the beginning; 3) retell the third part of the story, the ending; and finally 2) retell the second, or middle part, of the story. This middle part is what is left of the story after parts one and three are identified.

Retelling a story is easier when students have a guide, such as a graphic organizer, to help organize their thoughts and ideas. Give ◀ students a copy of the **Easy as 1, 3, 2! reproducible (page 61)**. Encourage them to use this organizer to help put their thoughts about the story in order. Remind them that they don't have to use full sentences, only words and phrases. They will use their organizers to rewrite the story on a separate piece of paper.

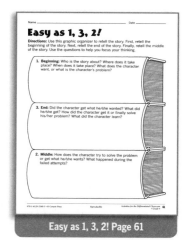

Easy as 1, 3, 2! Page 61

Easy as 1, 3, 2!

Directions: Use this graphic organizer to retell the story. First, retell the beginning of the story. Next, retell the end of the story. Finally, retell the middle of the story. Use the questions to help you focus your thinking.

1. **Beginning:** Who is the story about? Where does it take place? When does it take place? What does the character want, or what is the character's problem?

3. **End:** Did the character get what he/she wanted? What did he/she get? How did the character get it or finally solve his/her problem? What did the character learn?

2. **Middle:** How does the character try to solve the problem or get what he/she wants? What happened during the failed attempts?

Aesop to the Rescue!

Standard

Read a wide range of literature from many periods in many genres to build an understanding of the many dimensions of human experience.

Objective

Students will practice determining the morals of stories.

Materials

copy of Aesop's fables

Teach students to look for the meaning, or theme, of a story. Here are a few quick focus activities using Aesop's fables to help students focus.

- Write the morals of three of Aesop's fables on the board. Read aloud one of the three fables. Then ask students to match the moral to the fable and explain why it matches.

- Read a fable to students. Challenge them to explain the moral in their own words.

- Give students a moral from one of Aesop's fables, and challenge them to work with a partner to illustrate the moral with a brief, original story.

- Give students a list of Aesop's morals. Ask them to rewrite the morals in their own words.

- Invite student pairs (or small groups, depending on the number of characters) to act out one of Aesop's fables. At the end, one student explains the moral of the story.

After completing these activities several times, students will be accustomed to identifying the moral of a story and will be able to recognize a variety of themes in literature.

What is the moral of the story?

Catch and Release

Standard

Apply a wide range of strategies to comprehend, interpret, evaluate, and appreciate texts.

Objective

Students will play a game to practice proving a main idea by providing supporting details.

Materials

soft, squishy ball

Strategy

Rehearsal

When discussing characteristics of a character in a story or when reviewing information for a test, students often perform better on their toes, moving and thinking! Movement stimulates blood flow to the brain and appeals to kinesthetic learners.

Catch-and-release is a policy where fishers release some or all of the fish they catch in order to sustain fish populations. In the classroom, it is the name of a game in which students must catch a ball and then release information. This game helps students review the concepts of main idea and details.

1. To play the game, move to an area of the classroom that is free of desks and other possible hazards. Ask students to stand in a circle around you. (You can also have students stand at their desks while you stand at the front of the room.)

2. Begin by stating a main idea from a story students are reading. For example, if students are reading *Charlotte's Web*, you might say: *Templeton is a selfish rat.* Then toss the ball to a student.

3. The student's job is to give a detail that proves or supports your main idea. The detail must be a complete sentence. For example: *Templeton would rather eat Wilbur's food than help Wilbur.*

4. The student then tosses the ball to another student, who must give another detail. For example: *Templeton only helps Wilbur if he gets something in return.* If a student gets the ball and doesn't know what to say, prompt him or her by appealing to the whole class. Ask students: *What is another detail for this main idea? What else do we know about this character? What did we forget to include?*

5. The game continues with you providing main ideas and students providing supporting details until you've covered the desired material. You can ask students to provide main ideas, as well.

Catch and Release is great for test or content review for any subject. For example, use main ideas such as:

- *A person must do several things to become a U.S. citizen.* (Students must list what the person must do to become a citizen.)

- *The product of two negative numbers is a positive number.* (Students must give examples such as: *The product of negative 8 and negative 4 is 32.*)

Ideas for More Differentiation

When stating main ideas, make sure to consider different readiness levels and provide easier and more difficult ideas. This provides more opportunities for student success. Allow students to respond by raising their hands, or make sure to throw the ball to students who can succeed at that level.

Extra, Extra, Read All About It!

Standard
Use spoken, written, and visual language to accomplish a purpose.

Objective
Students will work in cooperative groups to create a class newspaper.

Strategies
Cooperative group learning

Adjustable project

Informing parents of what happens in the classroom is an important part of a teacher's job. When parents ask their children, *What did you do in school today?*, the common response is, *Nothing!* What better way for students to communicate everyday classroom happenings than to write a class newspaper?

Have students work in cooperative groups to create a newspaper that tells what is going on in your classroom. Assign each group a section of the newspaper based on their talents, interests, and abilities. Newspapers can reflect subject matters taught in class: math news, reading news, science news, PE news, and so on. You may also want to include a comics section, a food section (detailing the latest culinary feasts found in the cafeteria), an editorial section (where students can write their opinions about various classroom and school activities and rules), an upcoming events section (that gives information about school events such as Open House, concerts, and holiday shows).

Organize groups by their levels of skill, comfort, and interest. For example, some students are better at writing, and some enjoy drawing. Students who are good at putting things together might like to lay out the newspaper. Interpersonal learners may like conducting interviews, while others may enjoy working on the computer.

Each group will publish its section in the required format. Perhaps students are skilled in desktop publishing, or they can simply handwrite it. Publish your newspaper in the format that works best for your classroom. You may choose to photocopy newspapers and send them home with students every week, or you can e-mail newsletters to parents.

Character Chat

Strategies

Rehearsal

Role play

Standard

Apply a wide range of strategies to comprehend, interpret, evaluate, and appreciate texts. Draw on prior experience, interactions with other readers and writers, knowledge of word meaning and of other texts, word identification strategies, and understanding of textual features.

Objective

Students will write a list of questions for different characters in a story and then role-play those characters to answer the questions.

Tell students to imagine what it would be like to have lunch with their favorite story character. Ask them: *Whom would you invite, and why? What kinds of things would you discuss with this character? What questions would you like to ask?*

Invite students to work individually or in pairs to write a list of questions for their favorite character in a story or novel the class is reading. The questions should be written so the character can actually answer them. For example, you couldn't ask Charlotte the spider in *Charlotte's Web: What's your favorite movie?* The question wounldn't work because she didn't go to the movies. A good question for Charlotte might be: *What do you think will happen to Wilbur after you're gone?*

Once students have generated a list of questions, gather volunteers who would like to play those characters. Arrange chairs in the classroom to look like the set of a television talk show. One student acts as host and asks each guest the questions. The guest, or student playing the character, must answer the questions as the character might. Encourage students to role-play these characters as accurately as possible, using special voices, accents, or expressions.

Get the audience (the other students) involved, too! Invite the audience to ask questions or ask for clarifications of the guest's answers.

Comprehension Strategies: Predict, Infer, Conclude

Standards
Apply a wide range of strategies to comprehend, interpret, evaluate, and appreciate texts.

Draw on prior experience, interactions with other readers and writers, knowledge of word meaning and of other texts, word identification strategies, and understanding of textual features (e.g., sound-letter correspondence, sentence structure, context, graphics).

Objective
Students will use a graphic organizer to interact with text.

Materials
Predict, Infer, and Conclude reproducible

Students are often asked to predict, infer, and draw conclusions when studying different texts. However, they may not understand the difference between these skills, which are essential to analyzing text. Use the **Predict, Infer, and Conclude reproducible (page 68)** to help students better understand the difference between these three reading skills.

Begin by defining each skill for students, and provide an example.

Predict: To state what you believe will happen based on known facts.
*I **predict** that my friend will love the new green sweater I got her for her birthday because she's always cold, she wears a sweater to school every day, and her favorite color is green.* (Nothing has happened yet. The prediction is based on known facts.)

Infer: To arrive at a decision or opinion based on known facts or evidence.
*I **infer** by the smile on my friend's face that she loves her new green sweater.* (Something has now happened. The friend is smiling. An inference can be made based on the evidence of the friend's smile.)

Draw Conclusion: To use evidence and reasoning to state the final, logical result.
*I **conclude** that my friend loves her new sweater because she wears it to school every day.* (All the evidence is in. A logical conclusion can be drawn.)

These three strategies are all based on evidence; none is based on random thoughts. Invite students to use the graphic organizer to write their predictions, inferences, and conclusions about a specific text and to write the evidence used in making these decisions.

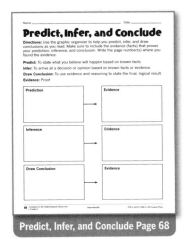

Predict, Infer, and Conclude Page 68

Name _____ Date _____

Predict, Infer, and Conclude

Directions: Use the graphic organizer to help you predict, infer, and draw conclusions as you read. Make sure to include the evidence (facts) that proves your prediction, inference, and conclusion. Write the page number(s) where you found the evidence.

Predict: To state what you believe will happen based on known facts.

Infer: To arrive at a decision or opinion based on known facts or evidence.

Draw Conclusion: To use evidence and reasoning to state the final, logical result.

Evidence: Proof

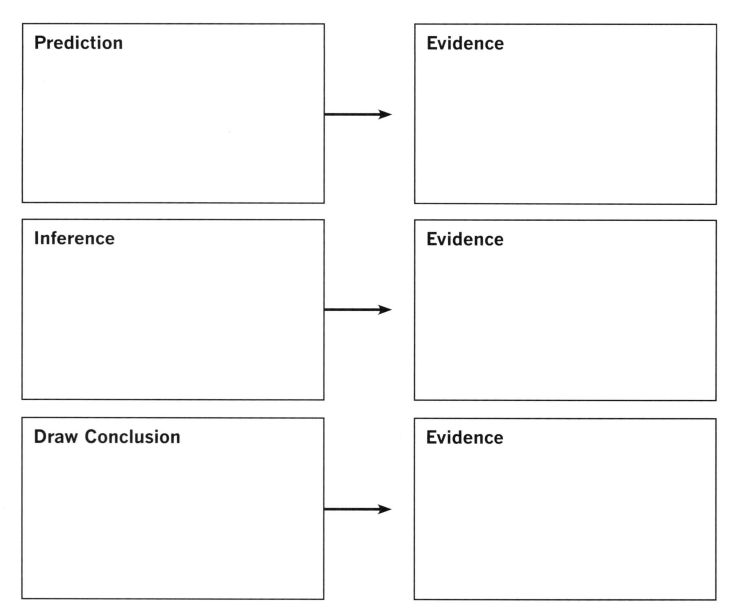

Comprehension Strategy: Evaluation

Standard
Participate as knowledgeable, reflective, creative, and critical members of a variety of literacy communities.

Strategy
Data board

Objective
Students will evaluate books and share those evaluations with their classmates.

Materials
Book Review reproducible

To *evaluate* means to decide the worth or quality of something. How often do students evaluate movies, video games, books, and music casually and effortlessly in conversation? However, when asked in class to evaluate a book they've read, students usually say, *It was okay, I guess.* Perhaps students don't effortlessly evaluate books in class because they're asked to evaluate assigned reading material. In order to motivate students to evaluate their reading, create an authentic environment of consumerism.

Word of mouth is a gold mine for companies because it's free advertising. When a product is good, word of mouth spreads the news, and the product disappears off the shelves. Likewise, when a product is not good, word-of-mouth can reduce sales. You can use this same strategy in your classroom.

Create a Book Review bulletin board where students can use word of mouth to evaluate and state their opinions about the latest, greatest library books or other chosen readings. Before going to the library, students can check the board before to see what their classmates thought about various books. This board is sure to inspire dialogue among students, such as, *You really liked that book, so I thought I'd read it too. This is the most exciting book I ever read! What is your favorite part? This book was so boring I could barely get through the first chapter.*

Students will be evaluating books without even realizing they are doing so. Give students several copies of the **Book Review reproducible (page 70)** to keep in a reading folder. Whenever they read a book they've enjoyed or disliked, they can share their opinions with classmates by filling out this form and posting it on the Book Review bulletin board.

Book Review Page 70

Book Review

Directions: Use this form to evaluate a book you read.

Book Title: _____

Author: _____

Evaluation Scale

(Circle a number that shows your opinion of the book. 1 means the book was awful; 5 means the book was great!)

1   2   3   4   5

Topic (What was the book about?)

_____

_____

What emotions did the book make you feel?

_____

_____

Did you look forward to reading it, or did you want to trade it in? Why?

_____

_____

What was the best or worst part of the book?

_____

_____

Would you give this book to a friend to read? Why or why not?

_____

_____

Comprehension Strategy: Questioning

Standard
Use spoken, written, and visual language to accomplish a purpose.

Objective
Students will use a questioning cube to formulate questions about their reading.

Materials
Questioning Cube reproducible
construction paper
tape
scissors

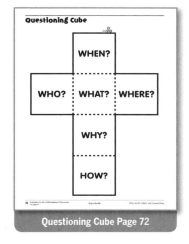
Strategy
Cubing

Students are always asked to answer questions. Get students to stretch their thinking by letting them do the asking! In order to ask meaningful questions, students should understand that there are different types of questions. Some questions have answers that are easily found in the text. Some questions have less apparent answers and are found in subtext or in the reader's own inferences.

Cubing is a great strategy for asking questions. Copy the **Questioning Cube reproducible (page 72)** on construction paper. Cut out, fold, and tape the shape to make a cube. (You may choose to make one cube for the whole class or several cubes for small groups.) The questioning cube has the simple question words *who, what, where, when, why,* and *how.* These words can begin questions with answers easily found in the text, or they can begin higher-level thinking questions.

For example:

- **When** *was the main character born?*

- **When** *did the main character start to feel that her friends were tricking her?*

- **Where** *did the story take place?*

- **Where** *was the sorrow the father was supposed to feel for his son?*

To elicit good questions from students, first decide if you want them to ask easily answered questions or higher-level thinking questions. Toss the cube to a student. Whichever word is on top is the word with which he or she begins a question. This is a great way to review material before a test!

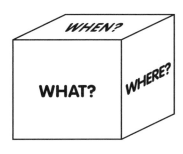

Questioning Cube

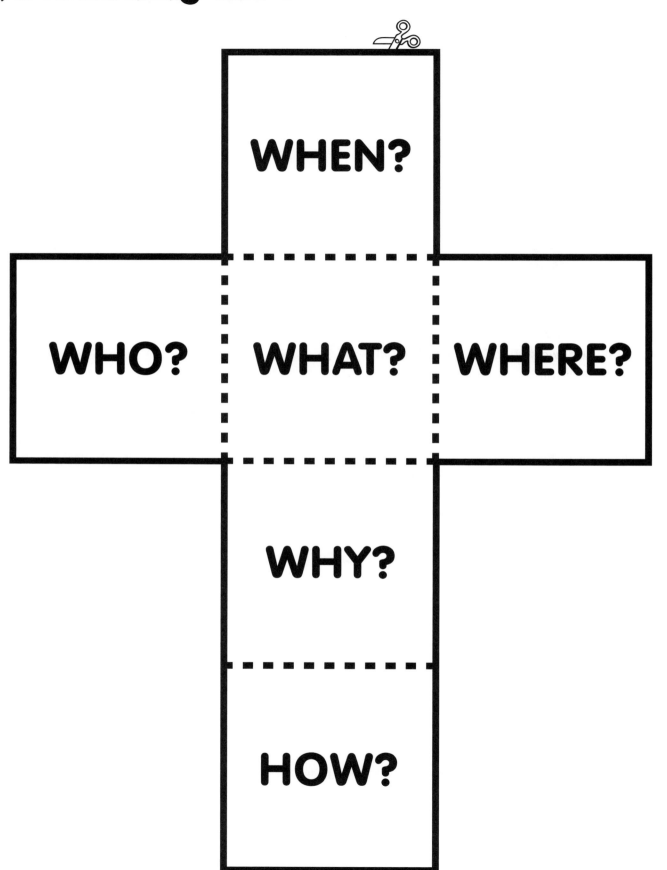

WHEN?

WHO? WHAT? WHERE?

WHY?

HOW?

978-1-4129-5340-5 • © Corwin Press

Comprehension Strategy: Compare and Contrast

Standard

Apply a wide range of strategies to comprehend, interpret, evaluate, and appreciate texts. Draw on prior experience, interactions with other readers and writers, knowledge of word meaning and of other texts, word identification strategies, and understanding of textual features (e.g., sound-letter correspondence, sentence structure, context, graphics).

Objective

Students will use a graphic organizer to help them liken and contrast characters, events, and so on, in texts.

Students are often asked to compare two items or ideas to show their similarities and differences. However, they may be unclear about the difference between the types of comparison. Remind students that when they liken two things, they are looking for similarities. When they are contrast two things, they are looking for differences.

The Venn diagram is the most common graphic organizer used for likening and contrasting two things. However, it can be difficult to fit all the text in the intersecting circles. The **Comparison Chart (page 74)** provides more room for students to write their ideas.

Invite students to use the Comparison Chart to liken and contrast two characters in a story, two stories by the same author, two different authors, two settings in stories, and so on.

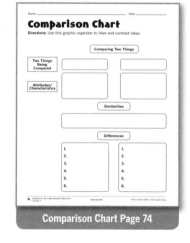

Comparison Chart Page 74

Ideas for More Differentiation

Allow visual/spatial, tactile, and bodily/kinesthetic learners to use two hula-hoops to compare objects such as shoes, or pictures of food or animals. Students can also work in pairs to compare features (e.g., eye color, hair color) or clothing.

Comparison Chart

Directions: Use this graphic organizer to liken and contrast ideas.

Comparing Two Things

Two Things
Being
Compared

Attributes/
Characteristics

Similarities

Differences

1.

2.

3.

4.

5.

6.

1.

2.

3.

4.

5.

6.

Noteworthy Expressions

Standard
Develop an understanding of and respect for diversity in language use, patterns, and dialects across cultures, ethnic groups, geographic regions, and social roles.

Objective
Students will work in center groups to make a list of expressions and their meanings.

Materials
sticky notes
drawing paper
colorful markers

When reading a book, English-language learners as well as English-only students often encounter idioms they find confusing. Help students understand this figurative language by doing the following activity.

1. As students read, encourage them to list figurative expressions such as idioms on sticky notes, one per note. They can keep the sticky notes on the inside cover of their book so they are always accessible.

2. After students collect several expressions, post the sticky notes on a wall by a table.

3. During center time, students can choose and write an expression on drawing paper and work with their center groups to figure out the meaning. Have the group use colorful markers to write the expression and its meaning and illustrate it. Soon, your walls will be decorated with colorful phrases!

If students can't figure out the meaning of an expression, they can use the key words *English idioms* to search the Internet. There are several Web sites dedicated to explaining idioms.

Ana was blown away by her Uncle's generosity = greatly impressed

Responding to the
Literature Response

Standard

Apply knowledge of language structure, language conventions, media techniques, figurative language, and genre to create, critique, and discuss print and nonprint texts.

Objective

Students will use graphic organizers to help them write literature responses.

Materials

In Response reproducible

When writing a literature response, students should demonstrate a clear understanding of the literature. They should make judgments and provide support for those judgments by using specific references to the text and their own prior knowledge.

Provide the following tips for students' literature responses:

• Remember the difference between a summary and a response. A summary is restating the author's main ideas. A response includes a brief summary and your opinions and ideas about the reading.

• Briefly summarize the story by explaining the big idea. This could be the moral or purpose of the story.

• Write your feelings about the author's main points. Do you agree or disagree? Or, why do you think the big idea is important?

• Give specific examples from the text to support your opinions. With what statements in the text do you agree or disagree?

• Connect the writing to your own life. How does the big idea relate to something that happened to you?

• Conclude your response by restating how you feel about the author's main points or big idea. Did the author support his or her main points? Is the author's conclusion logical? Did the story accurately illustrate the big idea?

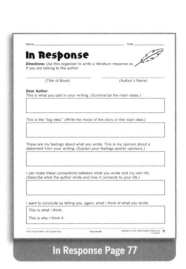

In Response Page 77

After reviewing the purpose of a literature response, give students
◀ a copy of the **In Response reproducible (page 77)**, which allows students to respond to literature in an easy, conversational manner. Students can use this organizer during the prewriting step of the writing process.

In Response

Directions: Use this organizer to write a literature response as if you are talking to the author.

_____   _____
(Title of Book)   (Author's Name)

Dear Author,
This is what you said in your writing. *(Summarize the main ideas.)*

```



```

This is the "big idea." *(Write the moral of the story or the main idea.)*

```



```

These are my feelings about what you wrote. This is my opinion about a statement from your writing. *(Explain your feelings and/or opinions.)*

```



```

I can make these connections between what you wrote and my own life. *(Describe what the author wrote and how it connects to your life.)*

```



```

I want to conclude by telling you, again, what I think of what you wrote.

This is what I think:

This is why I think it:

Finders Keepers

Standard

Apply knowledge of language structure, language conventions, media techniques, figurative language, and genre to create, critique, and discuss print and nonprint texts.

Objective

Students will use text to create a found poem.

Found poems are created using existing text. The text can be found anywhere—a newspaper, a textbook, a novel, or even a cereal box. Words, phrases, or sentences are taken from the text and then rearranged to create a poem. Found poems provide an unusual way to rehearse facts or synthesize information.

Before having students create found poems, consider the themes you're currently studying and books students are reading. Consider newspaper articles that relate to the theme as well as magazines, books, and Web sites. Then, invite students to create their own poems using one of the provided resources. It is relatively simple to write a found poem because the text has already been created. The poet's job is to choose parts of the text that appeal to him or her.

Have students use their resource to choose, rewrite, and arrange lines for their poem. Poets should not add any of their own words; words should only come from the text. However, punctuation and capitalization may be changed.

Example (using text from an oatmeal box):

Apples and cinnamon, banana, and maple
Quickly! Removes cholesterol!
MICROWAVE on HIGH
In an Instant
Reduce risk of heart disease.

Having students share their found poems is a great way to practice for a test or discover where more work needs to be done.

CHAPTER 5

Physical Education, Art, and Music

Centers for P.E.

Objective
Students will go to P.E. centers and participate in assigned activities.

Materials
6–8 hula-hoops
6–8 jump ropes
6–8 tennis balls
whistle
stopwatch

Centers provide students with the opportunity to work independently and accomplish tasks on a variety of skill levels. The key for P.E. centers is that three of them must be independent. While you are actively working at one center, you can monitor the other three.

1. Divide the class into four groups, one for each center: Hula-Hoops, Jump Rope, Tennis Balls, and Exercise. Send one group to each center.

2. The hula-hoop group works to keep hula-hoops going around their waists. The jump-rope group jumps rope, and the tennis ball group practices throwing and catching underhand and then overhand.

3. The fourth group is for exercises. You or an assigned student will lead the group in simple exercises such as stretches, toe-touches, waist-bends, standing on toes, jumping jacks, sit-ups, and so on.

4. After about seven minutes, blow your whistle. At the signal, students must drop their equipment and advance as a group to the next center. By the end of a P.E. period, students will have participated in all of the centers.

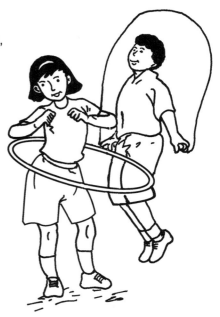

Heart Health

Strategy
Structured project

Objective
Students will learn how to take their pulse and compare heart rates before and after physical activity.

Materials
stopwatch

Heart health is an important topic for students at any age. Taking a pulse and understanding healthy heart rates is key to a creating a healthy exercise routine, now and in the future.

Checking Resting Heart Rate

Teach students how to find their pulse after they have been sitting quietly for a while. Show them how to use two fingers to touch the side of their neck next to their Adam's apple. They should feel the carotid pulse. Have students watch the clock for six seconds while counting their pulse. They then multiply that number by 10. That will give them the number of beats per minute of their resting heart rate. According to the Heart and Vascular Institute of the Cleveland Clinic, the normal resting heart rate for children ages 6 to 15 should be 70 to 100 beats per minute.

Checking Active Heart Rate
Next, have students go outside and run around on the playground. After they have been active for about five minutes, ask them to slowly walk back to you and take their pulse again. Use a stopwatch to count off six seconds. Have students multiply their new heart rate by 10, or just tell them to add a zero to the end of that number.

According to the American Heart Association: "Children are remarkably able to adjust their levels of activity to their individual capacity. The maximum heart rate in healthy children is about 200 beats per minute, and there is not need to arbitrarily restrict them to lower (target) heart rates."

Give students the following guidelines to help them gauge whether they are exercising correctly for maximum benefit:

- If you can talk a bit while exercising, you are doing well.

- If you are gasping for breath, you are working too hard.

- If you can sing, you need to work harder!

Line Soccer

Objective
Students will exhibit good sportsmanship while playing a game in which they try to kick a ball through a line of classmates.

Strategy
Game

Materials
soccer ball
beanbag or other marker
4 cones

1. Divide the class into two teams. Number each player so the same numbers are on each team. Position students in two lines about 50 feet apart, facing each other. Use lines already on a playing field, such as those for soccer.

2. Set up your playing field. Place the marker in the middle of the two lines, and place the soccer ball at the marker. Place one cone at each corner of the rectangle created by the two lines. These cones represent the outside boundaries.

3. Explain the rules of the game to students:

   The object of the game is to score points by kicking the soccer ball through the line formed by members of the opposing team.
   - To play the game, you will call out a number, for example, *seven!* The "seven" from each team attempts to kick the soccer ball through the other team's line.
   - The ball must not be kicked over anyone's head, and players cannot use their hands. (However, they may use their hands to protect themselves from flying balls.)
   - Team members who are not kicking the ball must stay on the line, but they can run along the line to keep the ball from passing through.
   - If the ball approaches a student on the line, he or she may kick it toward a teammate who is running the ball or to the other line. This student cannot run into the field and kick it. (This is where good sportsmanship is important).
   - When a ball gets past the line, the team that kicked it gets one point. The ball is then returned to the marker, and you call another number. Make sure to call all the numbers, so everyone gets a chance to score!

Obstacle Course

Objective

Students will use playground equipment to run an obstacle course.

The average playground usually has a couple of slides, a jungle gym, horizontal bars, and swing sets. Using your available playground equipment, create a simple obstacle course. If possible, have the course move in a circle or oval so students don't crash into one another while going from one piece of equipment to the next.

Choose the best way to move through the course. For example:

- Start at the big slide.

- Go down the big slide, and run to the jungle gym.

- Climb over the jungle gym, and then race to the horizontal bars.

- Cross the bars, and then run to the little slide.

- Go down the little slide, and then run to the swings.

- Swing 10 times, stop, and then run to the big slide.

- Repeat the course.

If you have a large class, start half the students at the beginning of the course and half of them at the middle. That way there isn't a long line of students waiting to get started.

Students need to exhibit their very best sportsmanship skills. Remind students that they need to wait for their turn, follow all playground equipment safety rules, and keep moving. Their heart rates will surely rise!

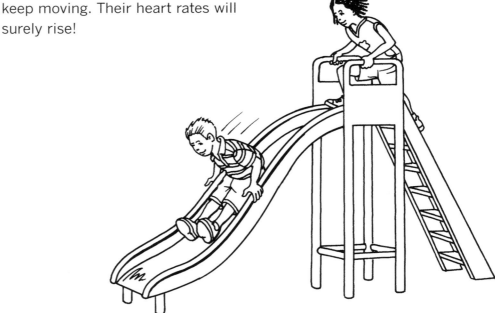

Kickball Basketball

Objective
Students will play a game involving kicking a ball and shooting baskets.

Materials
2 basketballs
2 basketball courts

This favorite game provides excellent exercise the whole class will enjoy. The game can accommodate a whole class, but students will get a better workout if the class is divided into two groups, one on each court.

1. On a court, group the players into two teams. (When creating teams, it's fun to use concepts from other content areas as team names, for example, *Herbivores vs. Omnivores.*)

   The Herbivores line up along the sideline of one half of the basketball court. The Omnivores scatter around the opposite half of the court.

2. Choose a pitcher from the Omnivores. Send your pitcher to the restraining circle in the center of the court. The Herbivores send their first kicker to the backboard opposite the Omnivores.

3. The pitcher rolls the ball to the kicker. The kicker kicks the ball in the direction of the Omnivores and then runs around the half court in a clockwise direction. (Older students may want to run the entire court.) See diagram.

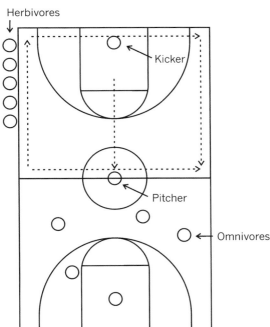

4. The Omnivores must capture the ball and then try to make a basket on their side of the court before the kicker can run around the half court and back to his or her backboard. If the Omnivores make a basket, the kicker is out. If the Omnivores do not make a basket, then the Herbivores get a point.

5. After three kickers are out, teams switch places. Continue the game until each student has a chance to be both kicker and pitcher.

Ideas for More Differentiation
Some students may not have the ability to participate in this game. Allow these students to be scorekeepers. They might also watch for fouls or signs of bad sportsmanship.

Color Wheel

Strategy
Authentic task

Objective

Students will make a color wheel in order to learn about colors and color mixing.

Materials

paper plates
tempera paint (red, yellow, blue, white, black)
paintbrushes
pencils
water to rinse brushes

Understanding concepts of color is not only important in the discussion of art but also in the development of color mixing and exploration skills. The basics of color can be found in a color wheel. This activity invites students to make their own color wheels to develop a basic understanding of color and color mixing.

Begin by explaining basic color concepts to students, emphasizing correct terminology:

- *Primary colors* are red, yellow, and blue. These colors cannot be mixed from other colors.

- *Secondary colors* are made when two primary colors are mixed.

- *Tertiary colors* are made by mixing two secondary colors, or by mixing a primary color with the secondary color closest to it.

- Adding white to a color to lighten it is called *tinting*.

- Adding black to a color to darken it is called *shading*.

Have students follow these instructions to make color wheels:

1. Draw lines on a paper plate to divide it into thirds.
2. At the edge of the inner circle of the plate, place a dab of red, blue, and yellow paint, one color on each line.
3. Between the primary colors, mix secondary colors. Mix red and blue to make purple; mix blue and yellow to make green; mix red and yellow to make orange. If time allows, continue mixing color variations, perhaps creating tertiary colors (e.g., mix orange and yellow to make yellow-orange).

4. On another paper plate, place a dab of black paint and a dab of white paint. Carry over some paint from the color wheel onto the black/white plate and experiment with tinting and shading.

5. When students are finished exploring colors with their color wheels, point out that complementary colors are found opposite each other on the color wheel. Thus, red is opposite green, blue is opposite orange, and yellow is opposite purple. These colors offer the most contrast to each other. Monochromatic colors are made from a single color that has been tinted or shaded. They offer the least contrast.

Ideas for More Differentiation

Invite students who love to write and describe things to continue to mix a variety of tertiary and monochromatic colors on additional color wheels. Encourage them to come up with creative and unique names for the colors, such as *rainy day, deep blue sea, burning flame, gooey green monster, and shining sun.*

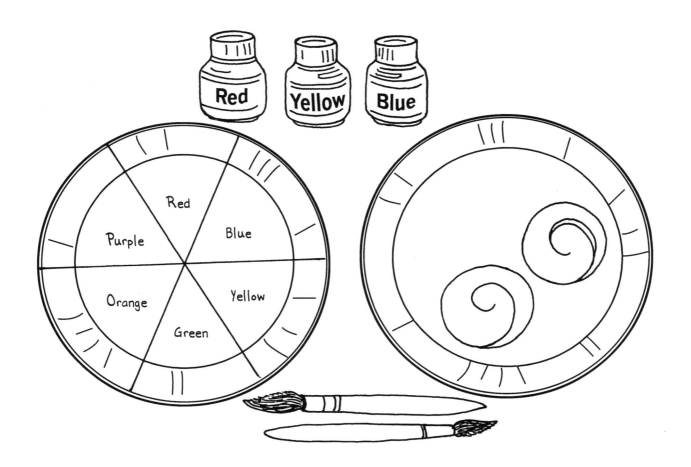

Van Gogh's Sunflowers

Strategy
Authentic task

Objective
Students will describe Vincent Van Gogh's brushstroke technique and use of color in his painting *Sunflowers*.

Materials
large print of Van Gogh's *Sunflowers*
real sunflowers
tempera paint (red, blue, yellow, black, white)
painting paper
paintbrushes
12" x 18" black construction paper
pencils
black, fine-line markers
water to rinse brushes

Once students have made color wheels (see page 84), they will be much more likely to understand discussions based on the use of color by artists such as Vincent Van Gogh. Use the following activity to help students explore colors and textures.

1. Allow students to study Van Gogh's painting *Sunflowers*. Don't provide a lot of direction; just ask them to look and think.

2. Begin asking questions, but direct students not to answer yet. Their job is to just look and think. Ask students: *What colors on the color wheel did Van Gogh use? Are they warm colors I or cool colors? If you were to touch the real painting, how do you think it would feel? Why do you think it would feel that way?*

3. After students have had a chance to think about the painting, elicit answers to the questions. Explain that Van Gogh used warm colors and thick brushstrokes to produce texture. Tell students that the use of thick brushstrokes is a technique known as *impasto*, the Italian word for dough. *Impasto* describes the surface areas on a painting that are heavily built up with layers of paint. An artist can put on layers of paint with a brush or a painting knife. Allow students to touch real sunflowers, especially the inner part.

4. To get a wonderful, close-up look at Van Gogh's use of impasto, go to the Web site of the National Gallery of Art in England, and search for Van Gogh's *Sunflowers*. Zoom in to examine the textures.

5. Continue your study of *Sunflowers* by having students count the number of flowers and study their stages of life. Some appear fresh, and some are wilting. Discuss what this might represent (the life cycle of a plant).

6. Finally, provide some background information about Van Gogh and his painting. Van Gogh used a lot of yellow, which he considered a happy color. He was excited about his friend Paul Gauguin coming to live with him in Arles, France. They were starting a colony of artists who would learn from each other. Vincent Van Gogh was Dutch. In Dutch literature, the sunflower stands for devotion and loyalty. Discuss what that represents, knowing that Van Gogh painted *Sunflowers* for his friend Gauguin.

7. To conclude your study, invite students to paint their own versions of this famous artwork. To get started, students will use pencil to draw the vase and flowers. Assist as needed. Tell them to begin by drawing the vase and the horizontal line of the table. Then have students choose one of the flowers in the middle to draw. Tell them to notice the direction that the flowers face (right, left, up, down). Some flowers have long, bent, pointy petals, and some petals are tight to the center of the flower.

8. Once the pencil drawing is finished, students can trace it with black marker. They will then prepare a paint palette with red, blue, and yellow paint, along with a plate of black and white paint for tinting and shading. Encourage students to mix their paints to make secondary and tertiary colors. They can copy Van Gogh's use of warm colors or decide to use a cool color approach. Allow students to use their own vision and creativity, but they should be able to describe their intentions, for example, *I've decided to use the cool colors blue and green to change the mood.*

9. After students paint their pictures, let their paintings dry overnight. The next day, they can retrace the flowers using black marker. Have students sign their name on the vase, just like Van Gogh did. Attach the pictures to pieces of black construction paper to frame them for display.

Meditation on Vegetation

Strategy

Exploratory center

Objective

Students will draw and paint a still life of vegetables.

Materials

6 or 7 strange-looking squash or gourds

plain tablecloth

crayons

painting paper

watercolors or thinned tempera

Tell students that they will be creating a still life using the crayon-resist method. This method consists of drawing a picture with crayons using hard pressure and then painting over it with a thin paint wash. The wax in the crayon will resist the paint, and the paint will fill in any uncolored paper.

1. Begin by arranging a still life of squash (the kind with all the bumps and colors) on a table at the art center. Drape a tablecloth around the vegetables.

2. Invite students to visit the art center. They should choose a specific point of view in order to maintain a certain perspective. They should not touch or rearrange the still life. If students don't finish their artwork in the first sitting, they should return to the same spot to finish.

3. Instruct student to use crayons to carefully draw the vegetables from their perspective. Encourage them to take their time drawing the texture of the vegetables, including bumps and grooves. Have them use appropriate colors to represent the vegetables and the tablecloth. Tell students to use hard pressure when coloring. For the background of the picture, they can use color or lines (e.g., wavy lines, dots).

4. When students are finished coloring, they will go to another table to "wash" the picture with paint. Encourage them to choose a color that complements their drawing. Display students' paintings around the classroom.

Everyday Art

Objective

Students will describe and discuss art in the world around them.

Strategy
Focus activity

Students are surrounded by art in their everyday lives. Use the following focus activity to help students understand that art is something beautiful and thought-provoking.

1. To get your discussion started, show students a Campbell's soup can. Explain that an artist named Andy Warhol painted pictures of soup cans. (Search on the Internet using the key words *Campbell's soup can art.* Andy Warhol's name will pop up. Visit some of these web sites to see pictures of Warhol's artwork.)

2. Tell students these pictures now sell for millions of dollars. Invite them to discuss why the soup-can picture is considered art but the can itself is considered just a can of soup.

3. Access the National Public Radio web site (www.npr.org) to find the article "Warhol-Signed Soup Can: Art or Memento?" by Kitty Eisele. This article describes a person who has a soup can with Andy Warhol's signature. A museum curator told him that it was a memento, not art. In order for the can to be art, the artist has to intend for it to be art. Discuss this story with students, and prompt students to respond.

4. Discuss that the use of line, color, positive and negative space, and so on, can be combined in unique or unusual ways to create art. To most people, a soup can is just a soup can. However, when Andy Warhol painted this familiar item, it was no longer just a soup can, but a symbol of home, family, comfort, and even the United States of America.

5. Ask students what they see when they look at the soup can. How about a box of cereal or a cat food bag? How about the doodles on the front of a school folder? What wonderful discussions will ensue in your classroom!

Ideas for More Differentiation

Instruct students to look around their world (e.g., neighborhood, house, backyard) for something beautiful, thought provoking, or artistic. Invite them to bring in, describe, or draw a picture of this item to share with the class. Ask student to tell what they thought was artistic about it.

Tree Study

Strategies

Authentic task
Journaling

Objective

Students will draw a tree using different kinds of lines and then reflect on their experience in a journal.

Materials

The Giving Tree by Shel Silverstein
drawing paper
pencils
clipboards

1. Read *The Giving Tree* to students. Then have students respond to the story in their journals. Prompt them with questions such as: *How did it make you feel? What is your opinion of the boy in the story? Did your opinion change when he grew into a man? What is your opinion of the tree? Does the tree remind you of anyone?*

2. After students have responded to the story, invite them outside to find a tree on the school grounds or in the surrounding neighborhood. (If you don't have ready access to trees, bring in books with pictures of real trees, or access images on the Internet.) Give each student a clipboard with drawing paper and a pencil for sketching.

3. While students are studying their chosen tree, introduce the concept of lines in art. Explain that lines can be thick or thin. They can be whole, broken, or jagged; straight or curved; or vertical, horizontal, or diagonal. Tell students they will use different kinds of lines to draw the tree. Encourage them to get close enough to examine the texture of the bark and leaves. Then challenge them to recreate that texture.

4. When students are finished drawing, bring them back to the classroom. Have them write in their journals to describe how they felt while drawing the tree. Prompt students with questions such as: *Did you think about* The Giving Tree? *Did you connect with the tree in some way? What did you learn from this experience?*

5. Display students' tree drawings around the classroom. Compare the different drawings of the same tree, and invite students to share their thoughts.

Clapping Patterns

Objective
Students will follow a clapping pattern after you.

Materials
drumstick (e.g., piece of dowel or ruler)

Learning and practicing effective listening skills is essential for students at any age. If students are listening effectively, they are actually hearing and thinking about what you say. To reinforce listening skills, try this sponge activity. This is a great activity for when you just have a few extra minutes or right before a lesson to get everyone's attention.

For this simple activity, all you have to do is clap a rhythm or pattern (e.g., *clap, clap, clap-clap-clap*) or use the drumstick to tap it out. Challenge students to repeat the pattern after you.

Vary the pattern, and use the stick to tap on different objects to make different sounds (e.g., your desk, a jar, a metal chair leg). Ask one student at a time to repeat the pattern. Then hand the stick to a volunteer, and let him or her create a new pattern.

For more challenge, invite students to repeat several different patterns back to back. Start with one, and then progress to two, three, or four until students can't remember the patterns anymore. This will really challenge their listening skills and concentration!

Foley Fun

Strategies

Cooperative group learning

Structured center

Objective

Students will record a story and create sound effects to support the reading.

Materials

tape recorder
blank audiotapes
stories for recording
found objects

A Foley artist is someone who adds sound effects to a filmed or taped performance. In this activity, students have the opportunity to use their imagination and creativity as they record themselves reading a story and making sound effects to make the story come alive.

To promote student interest and excitement about this activity, play a sound effects CD or tape for students. You may also access various sounds on the Internet. Ask students to guess what might be making the sounds. Tell them that in commercials, the sounds they hear are probably not what they think. For example, to make the sound of a steak sizzling on a barbeque, a Foley artist might record plastic wrap crinkling.

Invite students to work in cooperative groups at a structured reading center. In the center, provide a variety of materials students can use to make sound effects (e.g., aluminum foil, plastic wrap, spoons, different-sized pots, bottles, pie pans, hard-soled shoes, bells, whistles, cans, dried beans, paper lunch bags). Set up the center in a quiet corner of the classroom so students have a place to record away from normal classroom noise.

Together, group members will decide on a story to read. They can either choose one reader or decide to each read different characters' lines. Students will then analyze parts of the story to emphasize using sound effects. Part of the fun is figuring out which materials will create the sounds they want. Students will need to rehearse several times before they record.

Give each group ample time to gather their materials and record their stories and sound effects. Keep student tapes in a listening center for all to enjoy!

Instrumental Insight

Objective
Students will explore a web site that allows them to learn about different musical instruments.

Strategy
Focus activity

Most students can identify a piano and a guitar, but they may not be able to identify other instruments, such as a French horn, cello, saxophone, or oboe. They also probably can't associate the sounds they hear in music to the instruments that make them. Allow students to explore the Internet to learn more about musical instruments.

To gain student attention and interest, begin by playing Prokofiev's *Peter and the Wolf* for students. Challenge students to close their eyes, listen very carefully, and try to visualize the instruments they are hearing. After playing the music, ask volunteers to guess which instruments they heard.

Allow students to explore the Internet (under your supervision) to learn more about musical instruments. Use key words such *learn about musical instruments.* One great Web site is Music Education at DataDragon.com: *http://datadragon.com/education/instruments/.* This site allows students to choose from strings, woodwinds, brass, or percussion instruments. Students can listen to music featuring the chosen instrument, read a description of the instrument, and see a picture of it. This web site also provides information about musical notation.

To close your musical exploration, invite students to listen to *Peter and the Wolf* again. Ask students to see if they can better identify the musical instruments they hear. After this activity, it's likely they will be able to identify quite a few!

The Sounds of Music

Strategies

Think-Pair-Share

Journaling

Objective
Students will examine how music influences their lives.

In today's world of iPods, MP3 and CD players, radios, and televisions, music is all around us. Students can't imagine a world without music available at the touch of a button.

Share with students that just over 100 years ago, people did not have easy access to music. The only music people heard was created by their families and friends. If they happened to live near a cultural center, they might have the chance to hear music performed by an orchestra or a town band.

For this journal activity, invite students to write about the music they listen to every day. Prompt students with questions such as: *When do you listen to music? What kinds of music do you listen to? How do different kinds of music make you feel?* Allow students time to reflect and write.

Use the Think-Pair-Share strategy for a discussion about when and how people hear music. Ask students to think about what movies or commercials might be like without music. Initiate discussion with prompts such as: *What does music add to the telling of a story? Can music make a movie sadder, more exciting, or scary? Can you remember and sing commercial jingles? How does music make stories or advertisements easier to remember? Why does the music stick in our brains?*

Close the activity by having students listen to Prokofiev's *Peter and the Wolf* again. After each character is identified with its own music, challenge students to describe the character. Ask students: *How does the music for each character help you to see or understand him or her?*

Ideas for More Differentiation
Have students work in cooperative groups to develop music for a favorite story. Groups can assign characters or scenes to individual or pairs of students. Encourage creativity by allowing them to use found materials to make instruments, such as paper towel tubes, empty cans, dowels, bells, and so on. Invite one member of each group to read the story for the class while other members provide background music.

Moved by the Music

Objective
Students will listen to various types of music and move to express the way the music makes them feel.

Materials
variety of music CDs or audiotapes
CD or cassette player
crepe paper
streamers
tape

Music inspires movement! Get your students on their feet and moving by doing the following sponge activity. Students will be invigorated!

1. Give each student one long crepe paper streamer. The student can tape the end of the streamer around his or her middle finger or simply hold onto the end.

2. Tell students to spread out around the classroom. Explain that you are going to play different kinds of music. If the music's tempo is fast, they will move quickly. If the tempo is slow, they will move slowly. If the pitch of the music is high, they will elevate their bodies or hold themselves high. If the pitch is low, they will lower their bodies.

3. Tell students they are not allowed to touch each other, although they may move in and out of each other's space. Invite them to move the streamer around themselves to augment and accentuate movements.

4. Play different kinds of music, including various rhythms and tempos. Play multicultural music and some classroom favorites (preview all music for appropriateness). Play classical, country, rock and roll, blues, pop, rap, and even opera!

5. When students get tired, tell them to lie down on the floor. Then continue to play music, and ask them to interact with the horizontal space above them.

Ideas for More Differentiation
Be sensitive to those students who may feel self-conscious or embarrassed dancing in front of their classmates. Allow these students to move their streamers to the music rather than their entire bodies.

References

Cleveland Clinic Foundation: Heart and Vascular Institute. (n.d.). *Your pulse and your target heart rate.* Retrieved September 25, 2006, from http://clevelandclinic. org/heartcenter/pub/guide/prevention/exercise/pulsethr.htm.

Data Dragon Information Services. (n.d.). *Learn about instruments.* Retrieved August 10, 2006, from http://datadragon.com/education/instruments.

Eisele, K. (2006, May 9). *Warhol-signed soup can: Art or memento?* Retrieved September 25, 2006, from the NPR Web site: www.npr.org.

Gregory, H., & Chapman, C. (2002). *Differentiated instructional strategies: One size doesn't fit all, second edition.* Thousand Oaks, CA: Corwin Press.

Harcourt Brace social studies, grade 4. (2000). Orlando, FL; Atlanta, GA; Austin, TX; Boston, MA; San Francisco, CA; Chicago, IL; Dallas, TX; New York, NY; Toronto, Canada; London, England: Harcourt Brace and Company.

Harcourt Science California edition, grade 4. (2000). Orlando, FL; Boston, MA; Dallas, TX; Chicago, IL; San Diego, CA: Harcourt School Publishers.

National Council for the Social Studies. (2002). *Expectations of excellence: Curriculum standards for social studies.* Silver Spring, MD: National Council for the Social Studies (NCSS).

National Council of Teachers of English and International Reading Association. (1996). *Standards for the English language arts.* Urbana, IL: National Council of Teachers of English (NCTE).

National Council of Teachers of Mathematics. (2005). *Principles and standards for school mathematics.* Reston, VA: National Council of Teachers of Mathematics (NCTM).

National Research Council. (2005). *National science education standards.* Washington, DC: National Academy Press.